G000016391

Barcelona, Catalonia

A View from the Inside

by Matthew Tree

CataloniaPress
www.cataloniapress.com

Barcelona, Catalonia: A View from the Inside
by Matthew Tree

Published by Catalonia Press (an imprint of Cookwood Press)
http://www.cataloniapress.com
info@cookwood.com

Design, cover, and editing by Elizabeth Castro
Author photograph by Alba Danés

ISBN: 978-1-61150-006-6 (Print)
ISBN: 978-1-61150-004-2 (Enhanced EPUB)
ISBN: 978-1-61150-005-9 (EPUB)
ISBN: 978-1-61150-007-3 (Kindle/Mobi)

Contents

A Painless Preface   7

Life on the Receiving End   11

Columns   29

Bait	30	Skiving	50
A Free Ticket to Raw Fish	31	Mutton Dressed as Lamb	51
The Amazing Case of Jan Vardoen	32	England, My England	52
Day Trip to Limbo	33	Peply Conianes	53
Late One Afternoon	34	Lovelace, Linda	54
A Word to the Wise	35	Aftertaste	55
Much Ado About Nothing	36	Murder Most Foul	56
Plug Ugly	37	Fringe Deficits	57
Fever	38	Soapbox Blues	58
Driving Down	39	Just Try It	59
Kicking Against the Pricks	40	Bunch of C's	60
Moot Point	41	Something New	61
Success	42	Bane of Our Lives	62
Playing the Sage	43	Fifteen Minutes	63
Scare	44	A Prick in Time Saves Nine	64
All Right Now	45	Jungle Jinx	65
Return to Montserrat	46	We Know It's Christmas	66
Tough	47	Missionary Position	67
Israel	48	Bull from the Beeb	68
All the World's a Nationalist	49	Son of a Bitch	69

Columns, continued

Let There Be Light	70	Crusty Scab	115
Nip and Tuck	71	Our Nour	116
Just Couldn't Cope	72	Barfalona	117
Carnival Schmarnival	73	Just Say Nothing	118
The Exit Sign	74	Say What?	119
Strangling Animals Is Just Fine	75	Temps Fora	120
Publishers Be Damned	76	Najat	121
Blighty	77	Sweet	122
Gat Flap	78	Not Quite a Fight	123
A Wing and a Prayer	79	Self-Sold Man	124
The Rain in Spain	80	Lit Up	125
Round the Table	81	Flaming Amis	126
Freefall	82	Catchwords	127
Butchering the Idiot	83	Shop 'Til You Droop	128
Steal This Newspaper	85	Eventless	129
Tita in Denial	86	Game Not Over	130
Seven	87	Weird Doings	131
The Enormity of the Tragedy	88	Calling a Turd a Turd	132
Into Africa	89	Lifting the Lid	133
Eco-Pests	90	Unforgettable	134
The Unhappy Rock	91	Franki Goes to Can Brians	135
The Tanzanian TV Interview	92	On Hold	136
Africans Wear Watches, Too	93	If Only We Knew	137
Tour de Dunce	95	Blue Velvet	138
Frankly, My Dear	96	Losing the Game	139
Wedding Hell	97	Shut It	140
Love is the Dope	98	The Way They Were	141
Catalland	99	The Place	142
Saying Goodbye to God	100	Oh Ay	143
S.O.S.	102	Dawning of the Age	144
Mirror, Mirror	103	Hair Yesterday	145
If It Works, Don't Touch It	104	Small Train Coming	146
Rude Boys	105	Brushed Off	147
Then We Took Berlin	106	Dear Oh Dear	148
Grand Hotel	107	Pocket Pickings	149
How Does It Feel?	108	Crying Shame	150
Bad-Being	109	That's Entertainment	151
All the Time	110	Yakkety Yak	152
Out of Spirits	111	The Lost Nois	153
It's That Man Again	112	Don't Mention the War	154
Not in Front of the Foreigners	113	Hollow Tales	155
Socks	114	Lost	156

Matthew Tree

Columns, continued

Life Without	157	Passport to Arenys	171
Forked Tongue	158	No Flowers	172
Cupboard Love	159	Quim Monzó: A Profile	173
Finko, Finko, Finko	160	Najat El Hachmi: A Profile	174
The Day After	161	Before and After	175
More Con Than Mist	162	Space Cowboys	176
Guttersniped	163	Eyeless in Fraga	177
Teen Spirit	164	Andorra, Mon Amour	178
Pieces of Cake	165	Legislating the Obvious	179
Zora! Zora! Zora!	166	Summer of Hate	180
The Long Hello	167	Runaround	181
On Draft	168	Smokescreen	182
Beached	169	Year's End	184
Hootenanny Reunion	170	Harvest Time	185

Articles   187

Stranger in a Strange Land	188	Hard Times	208
Letter from Barcelona	197	Autumn of the Patriarch	210
Found in Translation	200	Waiting for the Break	212
Graphic Examples	202	Laughter in the Light	215
The Other Europe	204		
Catalan: An International Language?	206		

About the Author   219

A Painless Preface

Every now and then a world-shattering event comes along that takes everyone by surprise, not least the journalists and diplomats who are supposed to have their pricked-up ears pressed close to the ground. The Bosnian war, for example, caught them by surprise, as did the economic crisis that started to ruin millions of lives worldwide in 2009. The city I've lived in for the last 26 years, Barcelona, is almost certainly about to become the eye of another such hurricane, namely, the dissolution of the Kingdom of Spain as we know it, an event which will probably take place within the next decade, due to the secession of the as yet officially unrecognised country of which Barcelona is the capital: Catalonia.

For those of us long-term residents who've been standing on the tracks for nearly three decades, this particular train has been a long time coming. We've watched the attempts by successive Catalan governments to accommodate Catalonia within Spain's political structure by insisting on a degree of autonomy commensurate with the cultural reality on the ground; every single one of these attempts has failed. Spanish political power—Castilianised to the hilt—does not, apparently, wish to accept that there are live, contemporary, linguistically differentiated cultures within its remit. There is no point, it has therefore been argued, in trying to make pieces fit if the other player doesn't even admit that the pieces exist. If, to this political stalemate, we add a historically rooted belligerence—sometimes verging on xenophobia—towards the Catalans throughout monolingual Spain, and which has taken many forms, from throwing Catalans out of bars for speaking their language, through to nationwide boycotts of Catalan products, then the writing is clearly on the wall, as clear as the graffiti which appeared on Madrid walls during that unexpected Bosnian war: "Catalans, remember Sarajevo!"

If this news comes as a bit of a shock to English language readers, it is surely because they have been poorly served by their journalists, who, not speaking or even understanding Catalan, have voluntarily cut themselves off from much street talk, a bunch of newspapers and websites and blogs, a huge literature, and Catalonia's most listened-to TV and radio stations. Then again, this is only to be expected, given that these journalists, to a man and a woman, live and work in Madrid, a city where Catalonia, if it is mentioned at all, is regarded merely as a remote and troublesome province.

The material assembled in this book wishes to show part of the other side of the coin, being a collection of lectures and articles on different aspects of life in the Catalan capital, ranging from personal anecdotes and descriptions of some extraordinary incidents of anti-Catalan prejudice, through to summaries of the cultural scene.

When I first came into contact with Catalonia back in 1978, I was wary of the place—not believing that it really existed on the grounds that I, pompous young Londoner that I must have been, had never heard of it—until I realised I had stumbled across the cultural and social equivalent of a hidden treasure trove: perhaps the last trove of its kind left in Europe.

Despite my personal belief that Catalan independence would be a necessary boon both for those living within and without the borders of Catalonia, I am not a nationalist, which is to say, it would never occur to me to exalt a country irrationally (and much less violently) above any other, simply because I happened to be born there or just liked the place. However, I have been unable to avoid the undeniable fact that countries exist. After all, I was born in one, and I suspect most people have been too. Problems only arise when large numbers of people live in a country which is not stated on their passport. This has been the situation of the Catalans for many a long year. It is a situation which, as mentioned, many believe will not be going on for much longer.

These texts then, previously published in various English-language print magazines, newspapers and journals, wish to give one insider's view of pre-independence Catalonia: the only Catalonia, indeed, that any of us have known so far.

At least until the balloon goes up and the fat lady finally sings, I hope you enjoy the material that follows.

Matthew Tree, Barcelona, 2011

Columns

The following articles have been previously published in an independent, locally-based English-language magazine called *Catalonia Today*, which has a circulation of 15,000 and is read by a wide range of people, from tourists and foreign residents through to the English-speaking consuls stationed in Barcelona.

Bait

On Catalan-baiting

Catalonia Today 28 February 2006

Several months ago the Catalan parliament sent a proposal for a new Statute of Autonomy to the government in Madrid. As a result, a high-ranking military officer threatened Catalonia with armed intervention, Catalan goods were boycotted, and the Partido Popular launched a flagrantly disingenuous anti-Statute campaign, backed to the hilt by the Catholic-owned COPE radio station (whose passionate slandering of all things Catalan has proven a bit much even for the Vatican).

It needs to be said that none of this would have been possible had not important sectors of the population in Spain (outside Catalonia) already been suffering from a deeply ingrained anti-Catalan prejudice. I, for one, have come across numerous examples of this over the years, but none quite as unpleasant as two recent incidents, described by listeners calling into Xavier Bosch's morning radio programme on RAC1.

The first caller was a Barcelona taxi driver who had taken his (instantly recognisable) Barcelona taxi to Saragossa. Once there, he was insulted by other drivers, nearly had his car vandalised, and finally decided to leave the Aragonese capital when accosted by a gang of youths screaming *polaco de mierda! (Catalan shithead!)* The second caller was a woman from Sabadell whose teenage daughter had gone on a trip to Madrid with some school friends. In the metro, they were ordered to speak in Spanish (instead of Catalan) to each other, on the grounds that they were now "in Spain". When they refused, they were insulted and eventually threatened with violence by a patriotic young man who had to be held back by another passenger.

The curious thing is that the people responsible for this increasingly frequent Catalan-baiting are usually the first to insist that Catalonia does not have a national identity and is merely a region of Spain like any other. By their actions, however, they've managed to make Catalans travelling outside their native territory feel more at home in London or Lisbon, say, than any Spanish city you care to name.

Where is all this going to lead, I wonder?

Matthew Tree

A Free Ticket to Raw Fish

On a Peruvian restaurant in Barcelona

Catalonia Today, 8 March 2006

In a time when European teenagers travel to Asia, Africa, and the Americas at a drop of a hat, I sometimes find it embarrassing to admit that I am well past forty and have never been out of Europe. Slowly, however, this shame is going the way of all flesh as Catalonia becomes dotted with more and more food shops and restaurants run by members of what has gradually become a hugely diverse immigrant community. My stomach, at least, can now travel around the planet, without me having to move more than a kilometre or two from my Eixample flat.

This week, for example, I visited Peru for the first time (one stop on the metro) courtesy of the Cebichería-Marisqueria restaurant. Luckily, I was with friends who were regular customers (he Catalan, she Peruvian) because although the menu was written in Spanish, it was a Spanish liquidised over the centuries with Quechua (now the fifth most spoken language in Catalonia), not to mention Aymara and the numerous tongues of the Amazon. Not understanding a word, I stared, nonplussed, at dishes such as *cebiche, chicharrón*, and *papa a la huancaina* until my friends did the ordering for me and I discovered that *huancaina* was a yellow sauce served on baked potato, that *chicharrón* was fish (or octopus) fried in bread crumbs, and that *cebiche*—the Peruvian national dish—was one of the most delicious things I'd eaten for years: raw fish marinated in lime juice and served with chili, tomato, and thinly sliced onion. In the restaurant they had local Estrella beer, but I decided to stay in Peru and ordered Cristal, a fine, mild lager brewed in Lima. The Cebichería-Marisquería is on Rosselló, 530. As you can see, I'm plugging it for all it's worth, and it's worth plenty, and costs little, and it's like travelling without the jet lag. Go!

The Amazing Case of Jan Vardoen

On an old friend

Catalonia Today, 13 March 2006

Twenty-five years ago, when I first met him, Ian (as he still called himself) was living in a squat and on the dole in South London. He was a self-taught printer, locksmith, plumber, and electrician, skills he put to the service of the local anarchist movement, never charging a penny. His real ambition, however, was another kettle of fish altogether: he wanted, he said, to be a singer-songwriter. To which I would answer, trying to hide my scepticism, "Sure Ian, sounds great."

In 1989, Ian went to live in his mother's native country, Norway. Changing his name to Jan, he taught himself boatbuilding, cocktail mixing, and Norwegian. Ten years ago, when he visited me in Barcelona, he was working in a bar in a small town west of Oslo. He still insisted that his main ambition was to become a singer-songwriter. Sure, Jan.

Last week, I got a second visit from him. So Jan, how are things? He explained that eight years ago, in a run-down Oslo neighbourhood, he had been offered an equally run-down bar for peanuts. He bought it on a loan, then renovated it himself from top to bottom. It quickly became Oslo's most fashionable pub. He went on to open a restaurant, a delicatessen, and another bar. Noticing, perhaps, my incredulous expression, he showed me photos of these places. Then he put three books on the table. All in Norwegian, all by him. Two were about making cocktails, bestsellers both. The third was a collection of short stories. On the books he then placed four CDs. Also by him. Knocked down by his feather of a smile, I learnt that Jan had, on top of everything else, managed to become, at 43, a critically acclaimed singer-songwriter in his adopted country. It was a strange, exultant pleasure to discover that one of his finest songs, "Dressed In Black" (downloadable from *www.iansenior.com*) was about his anarchist days, when I first met him, twenty-five years ago.

Matthew Tree

Day Trip to Limbo

On the situation in French Catalonia

Catalonia Today, 20 March 2006

The French Government has long had a policy of condemning languages other than French to what might be called a jurisprudential void. (This once proved a boon to Henry Miller, who got away with publishing his US-banned *Tropic of Cancer* in Paris because, being in English, it was non-existent according to French obscenity laws.)

Oddly enough, this policy applies not only to foreign languages, but also to those spoken by many bona fide French citizens for generations, Catalan being a prime example. Last week I made a trip from Barcelona to Perpinyà (Perpignan, in French) and got a chance to see what happens when an entire culture is placed in legal limbo.

It was like stepping into an alternative universe. Here was the French equivalent of what Franco tried to achieve south of the border: a Catalonia reduced to the status of a de-culturised backwater. The only indication that a century ago almost the entire population was Catalan-speaking, were a few ratty-looking bilingual street signs in the Old Town. Catalan history, too, had been swept under the carpet, schoolchildren still being fed the myth of the Eternal Hexagon, without a mention being made of the fact that their home territory was annexed by Paris as late as 1659 and resisted its French occupiers for nearly 150 years.

Now, though, things are changing. Friends in Perpinyà, belonging to the one-third minority who still speak Catalan, assured me that their native tongue has recently become so prestigious that over 60% of the local population want their children to learn it. They are unlikely to do so, however, given that state schools in the area provide one hour of Catalan per week for a mere 15% of their students. Of course, older students can always learn the language in the nearby University of Girona. But to do so they have to apply, via Paris, for an Erasmus grant from Brussels. And there was I, thinking that the UE was all about letting state borders crumble into dust.

Late One Afternoon

On nearly throwing up in a television studio

Catalonia Today, 28 March 2006

Tuesday and it's off to TV3 to take part in the round table discussion which kicks off Albert Om's live afternoon show *El Club*. This week I'm paired with Joan Reig, drummer of veteran rock band *Els Pets*, which suits me fine because Joan and I get on well, partly, I suspect, because neither of us has really got used to being over forty. On this particular day, however, we have another thing in common, namely we are both sick as parrots, feverish and nauseous (probably some kind of Spring allergy, according to Joan). So, while waiting to go on the set, we quaff bucketloads of Font Vella in an attempt to keep our restless bile at bay.

At the round table we talk about a handful of recent events, including the world premiere of *Firewall*, starring Harrison Ford (who comes across as a right plonker, if I may say so, answering the reasonable query as to why he chose Barcelona for the premiere with: "Gee...I guess...uh...hell, I don't know.") Once out of there, our make-up swabbed off, Joan and I walk down the ramp leading to the exit, still sick as parrots, and I mention to him that for a moment I thought I was going to throw up in front of the cameras and Joan laughs and says that would have been like a punk performance, something the Sex Pistols might have done. I tell Joan he's right, but in my case I would've been at least twenty years too late.

Then he gives me an odd, expressive look, which says, clear as crystal, that we are both well aware that for quite a while (ever since we turned forty, in fact) neither of us has been able to get away from the unsettling sensation that whatever we produce now and in the future (a song, a book, a technicolour yawn on live TV), it is always, inevitably, going to be at least twenty years too late.

Matthew Tree

A Word to the Wise

On a new translation of Hans Christian Andersen

Catalonia Today, 3 April 2006

It was a surprise Christmas present: *Fairy Tales* by Hans Christian Andersen, in a new English translation (the best yet, according to Harold Bloom) commissioned for the Penguin Classics series.

Until I read it last week, I'd always thought that Andersen, like other well-known tellers of fairy stories, such as Charles Perrault, the Grimm brothers, or, closer to home, the Catalan folklorist Joan Amades, had limited himself to the transcription of existing folk tales. On the contrary, he invented plenty more off his own bat, including some that have become commonplace myths today, such as *The Ugly Duckling*. According to his biographer Jackie Wallschlager, this creative dabbling with popular lore constituted a major literary breakthrough, and not just for future kiddies' authors.

Reading this highly faithful translation, which puts paid to decades of insipid, flowery versions put out not only in English but also in German (and from these languages into most others), it is easy to see why Wallschlager is so enthusiastic. Andersen managed to conjure up an imaginative world as cleanly-honed, sharply-coloured, and all-embracing as that of any classic legend you care to mention. What's more, when reading these stories, with their talking teapots and queens with ice for flesh, far from slipping back into childhood, I found myself dwelling compulsively on the time-honoured universals—you know the ones (Woody Allen even spoofed them in a film)— love and death. In short, this is one wonderful book. If anyone gets hold of a copy after reading this article and finds it disappointing, they should write to this paper and I personally will send them a teapot that can't talk.

Much Ado About Nothing

On being published

Catalonia Today, 12 April 2006

Last week my eighth book—a diatribe called *La puta feina [Damn work]*—was published, and for the eighth time I am in the state I first experienced when the first book came out ten years ago: a quasi-neurotic restlessness akin to that of a lover who fears he's about to be jilted.

The process is always the same: first of all, the publisher praises the b'jesus out of the book (almost all writers get this treatment, as few publishers bother to bring out something they don't think is worthwhile; the catch is that their opinion is as fallible as anyone else's). The publisher then raises my expectations to the nth degree by assuring me it's going to sell like hot cakes (not unusual either, as most publishers desperately want this to happen).

No sooner has the thing appeared in the shops than I am on the prowl, cruising for readers' opinions with the alertness of a randy cat.

From here on in, my behaviour becomes increasingly erratic. If I know someone has a copy of the book, I scrutinise their body language for tell-tale signs as to what they think of it. I pester the sales assistants in good bookshops everywhere with questions about the book's progress. I check the bestseller lists on the internet at least three times a day. I bore my girlfriend stiff with a daily analysis of how the book is faring, based on all of the above.

In fact, there is absolutely no way I can tell at the moment if the book is going to sell or sink like a stone. Meanwhile, my fretting refuses to let up, as relentless—and about as interesting, now I think about it—as one of those never-ending drizzles that hit Barcelona around this time of year.

Plug Ugly

On a new type of ugly building in Barcelona

Catalonia Today, 29 April 2006

Pep's barbershop is on the corner of Aragó and Passeig de Sant Joan, in Barcelona's Eixample district. Every month or so, Pep gives me, at my request, the exact same flat-top. For the last eighteen years, this haircut has sat imperturbably on top of my head, pretending to take no notice of the rampant signs of aging in the face below it.

I was getting my umpteenth flat-top at Pep's last Saturday, and, and, and as is our wont, both of us had started laying into Barcelona's Mayor Joan Clos, whom we have no hesitation in describing as inept, clownish, and money-grubbing (and that's when we're trying to be kind). All of a sudden, Pep said, "Do you know they've gone back to building *afegits de Porcioles*?"

Porcioles was Barcelona's Francoist Mayor from 1957 to 1973. He was notorious for many things, not least for allowing the illegal construction of *afegits* or "added-on flats" on the top of some of the Eixample's most beautiful buildings. These 1960s-style eyesores were eventually removed under the mayorship of Pasqual Maragall some twenty years later.

Spurred on by my incredulous expression, Pep took me onto the street and pointed out the four plug-ugly penthouses that had recently been built within spitting distance of his business.

This time round, according to Pep, it is perfectly legal to put up one of these things: the City Council has special permits available for any citizen rich enough to afford them, and callous enough not to have any qualms about ruining one of the finest architectural conurbations in Western Europe.

On the bright side, maybe this return to Francoist-era town-planning will result in a scandal big enough to get Clos ousted from office. Should he finally resign under this particular cloud, remember, please, that you read it here first.

Fever
On being feverish
Catalonia Today, 30 April 2006

At the time of writing, I have spent the last five days at a constant temperature of 39°C (due to an infection the details of which I have no wish to go into). As I lay awake at nights, staring at the ceiling, vaguely troubled by the unopened mail next to the bed, it struck me that years ago, in similar situations, I had reacted very differently.

When I was in my twenties, for example, fevers would have me writhing around in my rented room in Poble Sec, imagining all manner of things in full technicolour.

On one occasion, for example, I sweated an entire anarchist rock opera into existence in the space of three of the small hours: the theme music, the funny bits, the dance routines, you name it. I had an entire black and red extravaganza going, all of it designed to show audiences around the country that anarchism was, really, the best option of them all. Sadly, the show folded for good as soon as its perspiring empresario finally nodded off.

On another, particularly bad night, a niggling feeling of jealousy towards my girlfriend at the time, who had just gone back to her native London, was mushroom-clouded by the fever into a hectic mesh of shadow scenes that jerked their way across all four walls, revealing her and an unidentified man humping away without fear or shame in front of my dilated eyes. (Later, as it turned out, I found out that I'd not only got the date right, but most of the positions as well.)

Twenty years on, however, I seem to be taking my fevers with a pinch of salt. As I said, this time round, far from imagining show-stopping scenes or bacchanalian sex, I merely stared at the ceiling and waited for the next thought that came into my head. The next thought turned out to be this mild little article, which only goes to prove my point.

Matthew Tree

Driving Down
On the founding of the Barcelona Ritz

Catalonia Today, 8 May 2006

Last Friday, the poet Joaquim Sala-Sanahuja gave me a lift from Farrera, a village of 23 people slapped like an afterthought onto the side of an otherwise untouched mountain in the Pallars region of the Catalan Pyrenees. As we drove down, Joaquim tapped into his all but unlimited knowledge of all things local and told me a handful of nearly unbelievable true stories.

There was the one about the first Catalan spiritualists, for example: mediums and table-tappers who the Generalitat placed straight into the shock units of the Republican army in 1936 on the grounds that as they didn't believe in death, they couldn't be afraid of it (the few survivors ended up sporting medals galore). Then there was the story of *Light of the Jungle*, a Catalan pre-hippy from the 1920s who lived in the open air in a field near Sabadell for sixty years (dancing naked every dusk and dawn) and then faked his death in 1981, thus giving himself the pleasure of reading his own obituaries in the Barcelona press.

Best of all, though, was the story of Tor d'Alòs, sheep merchant supreme of the Pallars and co-founder of the Ritz hotel in Barcelona. One day (this was in the early years of the 20th century) he paid his first visit to the restaurant at the Ritz, wearing his shabby merchant's clothes. The waiters refused to serve him. He came back in full evening dress, and ordered a plate of king prawns. When these were served, he smeared them all over his dicky and screamed at the staff, "In this hotel of mine I see it's the clothes that eat, not the people!"

Joaquim and I had hit the Diagonal by now, its lights spread out tacky as fashion jewellery. The crags of the Pallars seemed a world away. The Ritz hotel, however, was just over to the right. Within spitting distance, as it were.

Kicking Against the Pricks

On European ignorance of
Catalan language and culture

Catalonia Today, 12 May 2006

There he sat, in my flat, twenty-four years old, as well-informed a person as any to be found in Europe: he lived in a major capital (Amsterdam), had been through tertiary education, spoke four languages including his native Dutch, and regularly read the papers.

We met last year, not long before Sant Jordi's Day, which he'd heard of and wanted to know more about. Among other tidbits of information, I trotted out the fact that Catalan-language publishers sold over 30% of their books on that day alone.

He raised his eyebrows, frowned incredulously, leaned forward and finally said, "Catalan is a written language?"

After having spoken Catalan for nearly a quarter of a century and having read a fair amount of Catalan literature dating from the 12th century through to the 21st, I take it so much for granted that I am living in a normal culture I sometimes forget that out in the wide world, the vast majority of people, even "educated" Europeans, are so blissfully ignorant of things Catalan that, as far as they're concerned, all Catalan-speakers past and present (myself included) might as well have spent our lives stuffed away in cryogenic canisters.

It's no use explaining, for example, that Catalan is the seventh most-spoken language in the EU, the only one to be used in four different states and the nineteenth most-used language on the internet. None of this will convince uninformed foreigners that they should take Catalan culture as seriously as any other.

Many Catalans feel that this unilateral display of ignorance will only come to an end on the day when, upon being asked where they're from, they will be able to brandish a passport marked *Catalunya* by way of an answer. Even my Dutch acquaintance would then realise that Catalan is, at least, a written language.

Matthew Tree

Moot Point

On the watering down of the
new Catalan Statute of Autonomy

Catalonia Today, 15 May 2006

Spanish and Catalan politics have always been somewhat academic matters for me because although I've lived here for over two decades, I can't vote. This is my own fault entirely, given that I am a fanatic who refuses to apply for a Spanish passport on the grounds that I do not feel I am living in Spain. So I have ended up watching the comings and goings of the local politicos with a detached air, laughing at the slip-ups, frowning at the frequent abuses of power, and hoping, above all, that they won't do anything that might affect me personally.

However, the recent knock-on effects of the new Catalan Statute of Autonomy did manage to shake me up a bit. As I watched the right-wing party Convergència i Unió make a deal under the table with the Spanish socialists to accept a watered down version of this Statute, as I listened to chief Statute negotiator Alfonso Guerra boast that he had "planed the Statute right down" (the verb for *to plane* in Spanish being *cepillar*, which also carries a popular meaning of *to kill*), as I watched Esquerra Republicana—which prefers the original, unabridged draft of the Statute—being booted out of a government it had been instrumental in creating, I started to get a nasty feeling that we inhabitants of Catalonia had been roped into taking part in a huge, carefully scripted circus, designed to keep an audience of Spanish centralists from both the Left and Right in stitches.

There's an old anarchist saying, "If voting could change anything, it would be illegal." The Statute as it stands now, if accepted, will leave Spain as uniform (and as persistently begrudging to its internal minorities) as before.

So I am seriously considering getting a Spanish passport, for the sole purpose of voting a big fat NO in the imminent referendum.

Success
On being admired in primary school
Catalonia Today, 23 May 2006

I am well aware that it's considered tacky and tasteless to write about the cute, smart things that your own children do, but bear with me, I'll be as brief as I can.

Last week, at the (very good) local school my son goes to in the Fort Pienc neighbourhood of Barcelona, his teacher decided to run a memory test. She held up photos of winners of the Nobel Prize for Literature, recited their names, and then, a moment later, held up the photos again to see if the pupils, aged between three and four, could remember who was who. All went well until the turn came of a picture of a well-fed middle-aged man with no hair. There was a stunned silence. Nobody, it turned out, had a clue. Then, out of the blue, my son, who is only just beginning to talk, yelled, "Pablo Neruda!"

The entire class, the teacher included, burst out in spontaneous applause, leaving my son, evidently, pleased as punch. It was easy to see why for a few days afterwards he went about shouting out the name of the Chilean poet at the most uncalled-for moments: he was conjuring up this first taste of success.

A taste which comes whenever we do something that inspires admiration in other people. I've only really had the pleasure of this taste once, myself, but it has lingered on the tongue to this day. I was in Valencia, in 1999. My second book had been awarded the Premi Octubre de Narrativa. Relentlessly self-deprecating as I was at that time, when I climbed onto the podium to collect the prize and saw half a thousand people rise to their feet to give me a standing ovation, I felt a dizzying joy, an uncontrollable elation, a moment of almost perfect happiness.

A moment not so different, I imagine, from the one my son had last week, when he shouted *Pablo Neruda* in a room full of infants.

Matthew Tree

Playing the Sage

On being asked for advice by an aspiring writer

Catalonia Today, 29 May 2006

Last week I was in Sant Pere de Ribes doing what writers here optimistically call a *bolo* (gig): that is to say, a round table or an informal talk, as if our literary witterings before small audiences containing disproportionate amounts of sleepy senior citizens, could possibly be compared, excitement-wise, with even the most modest of rock concerts.

Anyway, after the talk was over, I was approached by a teenage girl who wouldn't have looked at all out of place in a rock concert, as it happened. She lingered at my podium table in what a nineteenth century author might have described as a charmingly hesitant manner.

She explained she wanted to be a writer, and needed some advice.

I felt a certain responsibility. Should I talk to her about imaginative integrity? Or about fighting against self-censorship? In short, about a few purely literary aspects of the trade?

Then I remembered what writing had really meant for me, roughly from her age on, for nigh on two decades: rejection. Novels rejected by publishers, stories rejected by magazines, month after month, year after year. At twenty-five, I managed to cover every square inch of the door to my room in London with rejection slips.

To her surprise, I blurted out, "Stubbornness! Don't stop writing, no matter what! Be stubborn!"

She thanked me politely and left, looking a mite disorientated. She would have looked more so, perhaps, if I'd added that even when you're published and the rejection slips are just a memory, you can't help feeling you're never going to be as good as you would like to be and will always therefore, consider yourself something of a failure. Then again, I thought, she'd find all that out herself in due time, assuming she was stubborn enough to last so long.

Scare
On being told I might have cancer
Catalonia Today, 4 June 2006

It started with a cold, about a month ago, which I smothered with an evil little over-the-counter product called *Couldina* (which includes codeine, a morphine derivate, among its ingredients). A week later, I stopped taking the *Couldina* and the cold sprang back with a vengeance, throwing in a nasty cough for good measure.

I went on hawking and sneezing for the next fortnight, and when the coughing got so bad it started to produce painful muscle contractions in my chest, I decided it was time to visit the nearest A&E.

The doctor sent me off for an X-ray to see if there was any bronchitis involved. Once he'd seen the pictures, he immediately ordered a magnetic resonance scan, after which I was placed in a small room and left alone for three hours. This, it turned out, was the time it took for the X-rays and scans to be analysed over the internet by a specialist at another hospital. By now, I was beginning to suspect I had something a little more serious than a cold.

Sure enough, when the doctor stepped into the room, he came out with the strangely familiar line, "I don't want to scare you, but the news is, frankly, not so good." He placed the X-ray of my chest against a light-plate, and pointed to a disarmingly large sphere floating at the bottom of the right lung.

This, he explained, might be a pocket of air, a benign tumour, or—and here he paused—a cancer. He urged me to see a pneumologist first thing Tuesday.

By the time you read this, I will have been told, I hope, what it is I have. If it turns out to be the worst of my three options, I promise not to talk about the approach of death in every succeeding column. On the contrary, I will talk about everything but. Life, I have just realised, is even more interesting than I had previously suspected.

All Right Now
On being told I probably didn't have cancer
Catalonia Today, 12 June 2006

Just on the off chance that anyone's been holding their breath since last week's article, in which I explained I was waiting to see a pneumologist who would tell me what the freshly discovered nodule inside my right lung was, I now have the answer: the pneumologist doesn't know exactly what it is (yet), but he's sure it isn't serious.

So I have stopped mentally writing the text I would have liked my children to read when they hit adolescence ten years from now, so they could hear the voice of their dead father rising up live and clear for the first and last time; I have stopped waking up in the small hours and playing my old friend Ian Senior's song about the London anarchists so that I could remember that good time in my life and say goodbye to it bit by bit, I have stopped fretting, in other words, about the possibility of the world—my world—being withdrawn from me within a period of six months to a year.

However, neither would I describe my feeling after being told I was off the cancer hook as one of unmitigated relief. On the contrary, I felt humiliated. I had been afraid. I had wailed out helpless laments at unexpected times. I had discovered I was not equipped to face off even a hint of death.

Death, by the way, when glimpsed close up, turns out to be a drab, persistent type in a grey mac who you know dislikes you intensely yet insists on keeping you company for purposes of his own (not unlike a man who tried to pick me up in a pub when I was fourteen). Although this time I have managed to make my excuses and leave, I now know full well he's still there in his corner, brolly in hand, his lips twitching out a friendless smile as he draws a bead on my back.

Return to Montserrat

On not believing in God

Catalonia Today, 20 June 2006

I hadn't been there since 1979, and all I recall from that visit is a large and smelly cafeteria that displayed endless dollops of *mel i mató* in its dessert section and someone trying to make me buy a bottle of Aromes de Montserrat, a liqueur which tastes OK if you drown it in ice and are already three sheets to the wind to begin with.

Since then, Montserrat has got quite cool. There's a brand new cafeteria with subdued lighting and reasonable food, a gift shop with an almost Ravalish trendy ethnic feel to it, and a bar normal enough for you to hang out there without anyone suspecting you're a Christian.

But above all, in my case, there was the prospect of meeting a real, live shitting monk, or at least a novice, which is the next best thing.

Efrem is a thirty-nine year old ex-schoolteacher who donned his habit after ten years of reflection. He turned out to be a witty, interesting man who answered all my questions, including a cheeky one about his sex drive, with a full-on honesty that would have disarmed the snidest cynic.

I didn't envy him his chosen way of life though. Not, at least, until he started talking about the days when he experienced moments of mystic elation, very similar, from what I could make out, to the kind of soda-like tingling I felt after my Anglican confirmation at age fourteen: a sensation that God was much closer to the skin than I'd ever suspected.

In my case, the bubble burst after six months, the buildings and paving stones of London came into sharp, crude focus, and suddenly God was nowhere to be felt. Since then, I have been a militant unbeliever. I listened to Efrem, however, with a growing yearning for that distant, brief period when I was convinced that I would have divine company right up until the day I popped the proverbial clogs.

Tough

On an old Barcelona friend

Catalonia Today, 25 June 2006

By any standards, my friend L. has had a tough life. She left school at four-teen, and has spent most of her working life in what she herself describes as dead-end jobs. She was brought up by a mother who wasn't good at showing affection—L. can't remember a single kiss—and a mentally backward aunt who died a few years ago.

At the moment, L. is having to cope with a series of problems on differ-ent fronts. Her mother has sunk into near catatonia, and is clearly on the way out. L. herself is taking medication for her recently-diagnosed hepatitis C. As if this wasn't enough, her boss treats her like a nincompoop, thus making her poorly paid job less bearable than it already is.

When I invited her round for the night of Sant Joan, she told me—without one iota of self-pity in her voice—that she was toying with the idea of putting an end to her life. She added she wasn't intending to leave her flat during the weekend.

As I insisted with a certain urgency, however, she did come round on Friday for a sip of *cava* and a bite of *coca*. Far from subjecting us to a litany of her ills, she was funny, cheerful, stoic, and wonderful with the kids to boot. As we talked, I remembered that this was the same L. who had fled from Horta to Menorca at eighteen to wash away a dreary adolescence, with whom I and other friends had had such good times in our late twenties (when we still clubbed through the small hours), that she was one of the very few people I find it easy to laugh with.

It dawned on me that L. has got over a hurdle many people fall at: she has proven herself imperturbably tougher than the life she has been dealt. All she needs now is to accept the fact that her friends love her more or less unconditionally, and I'd put good money on her soon becoming, well, happy.

Israel
On European attitudes to Israel
Catalonia Today, 26 June 2006

Now that something only just short of a full-scale war is taking place in the Middle East, we are all going to be hearing a lot of opinions about this small country; opinions which invariably prove to be subjective, often highly so, once their surface has been duly scratched.

For what it's worth, my own subjective opinion on Israel is influenced by two factors that I have found to be shared by very few people, least of all in Catalonia.

First, I have been reading about the Holocaust for many years and so have a fairly clear idea of what happened and when during Hitler's (and other leaders') war against the Jews.

Second, for four years I lived in a London flat chock full of Trotskyists who used to force-feed me their party line on the Arab-Israeli conflict, "The Israelis are doing to the Palestinians what the Nazis did to the Jews."

While recognising that the Palestinian plight was, obviously, a very real one, I pointed out that this simplistic reversal of roles was just not true. Take any slither of the history of the Shoah, and you will find atrocities of a magnitude that—fortunately—has not yet been seen in occupied Palestine.

However, some other oppressed peoples are getting something approaching Nazi treatment from their occupiers: the half a million Africans murdered in Darfur by Islamic militias, for example, or the ten per cent of the Chechen population liquidated by Moscow's military. To take just two recent cases among many.

I have often wondered why these events do not receive even a fraction of the scrutiny bestowed on the Arab-Israeli conflict. What have the Israelis got that the Sudanese *Janjaweed* and the Russian *spetznaz* haven't?

Answers on a postcard, please.

All the World's a Nationalist
On World Cup nationalism
Catalonia Today, 3 July 2006

Two weekends ago, the Raval-based group *Ojos de Brujo* played at an avowedly multicultural festival organised by Izquierda Unida in a village near Madrid. At the start of the concert, they mentioned they were from Barcelona, and were immediately booed. To avoid further confrontation with the audience, they eliminated further references to Barcelona from their lyrics; hence *las Ramblas* became *la calle* and so on.

(There is a certain irony to this, given that *Ojos de Brujo* have spent years telling us all that they are citizens of the world who belong to no nation, least of all Catalonia.)

This event took place as the World Cup continued to rage in Germany. I know there are people who watch the matches out of pure love of football, but it seems to me blindingly obvious that under the surface of the World Cup lies little more than an unashamed celebration of the most blatant nationalism we are ever likely to see this side of a war. All those people desperately screaming out the names of the nation states they happen to have been born in, depresses the hell out of me.

Not least because so many of the same people—and I'm sure we could include much of the audience that booed *Ojos de Brujo*—are capable of slagging off the Catalans on the grounds that the latter are *nationalists*. This is nothing more, say I, than an unusually stupid form of hypocrisy.

Which is not to say that the Catalans, like everyone else, aren't prone to a little bit of soccer-inspired nationalism themselves, despite not being allowed to have their own squad: on June 27th, each time France scored a goal against Spain, countless celebratory rockets exploded in the Catalan sky.

Skiving

On lousy restaurants in Valencia and Catalonia

Catalonia Today, 10 July 2006

We drove into Peníscola last Saturday, having been filming since 7 a.m. under a blistering hot sun, with no break for a snack. We were aching to eat, in other words. It was just Sod's Law, I suppose, that we ended up choosing the restaurant we did. An unpretentious-looking, medium-priced place.

It was empty, with not so much as a waiter in sight. When one appeared, twenty minutes after we'd sat down, our parched throats clamoured for beers. He nodded and disappeared again.

He came back over a quarter of an hour later with the drinks, an order pad and a jittery air about him (noticeable above all from his trembling hands and the thick bubbles of sweat that had appeared on his upper lip).

The average wait between courses being about thirty minutes, the meal took over four hours. Eager to escape, we got out credit cards. The waiter informed us with an apprehensive wince that the restaurant didn't accept them and then blurted out apologetically that everything had taken so long because it was his first day and the boss had left him and the cook to their own devices: no instructions, nothing.

We'd come across similar cases when eating on location in Valencia and Catalonia: lazy, absentee owners who couldn't care less about the problems of either staff or customers as long as the tills were filled at the end of the day.

These are the same owners who then complain about the chronic short-age of waiters. One of the discreet hallmarks of this country used to be the pride workers in the catering profession took in their jobs. Their employers, under the spell of that tired old sin Greed, are now making sure that such professionalism, like affordable rents and commission-free banks, is well and truly on the way out.

Matthew Tree

Mutton Dressed as Lamb

On British food labels

Catalonia Today, 29 August 2006

Possibly because I spent two whole weeks in England this year, instead of the usual one, I noticed for the first time that just about everything comestible there is labelled with adjectives as cute as they are hard to swallow. The sticker on a Tesco's "French sausage", for example, told me that it was "traditional, coarse cut, and dry cured". Which particular tradition? Just how coarse was that cutting? Sainsbury's goes one step further and, not content with informing us that their "British jester tomatoes" are "from the vine" (and not from the chicken coop or the tomato tree), adds that this product was "discovered" in the "Far East" by someone called Bernard Sparkes. Now, why would anyone in their right mind want to know that? Worse still, staples as familiar to the British public as crisps and pork pies have now become, respectively: "generous slices, cooked by hand", and "rich pastry filled with seasoned, cured pork". Dry cured, perhaps? Even pub menus have joined the adjectival bandwagon, offering things like Caesar salad with "shaved parmesan cheese". Shaved where?

May the Lord and all his angels keep this kind of verbal flim-flam out of Catalonia, where, like the local saying says, bread is bread and wine is wine. I punt. I have no idea why such baloney has proliferated so on English labels, but one thing's for sure: every time I go to London, after just a couple of days of eating the overwhelmingly adjectivised food which it is almost impossible to avoid there, I invariably get a violent attack of the squits that puts me off my beer, irritates my girlfriend, and ends up ruining the holiday.

England, My England

On the Americanisation of spoken English in the UK

Catalonia Today, 11 September 2006

This summer, in England, I spotted the flag of Saint George hanging in post office windows, flying from car windows, printed on trainers, sellotaped to house windows, and staring off countless T-shirts. I was astonished by this visual outburst of patriotism, unrivalled since the Union Jack fad of the 1960s.

Staunchly nationalistic, this display contrasted with the equally astonishing Americanisation of the language I was hearing all around me. A nurse in a London hospital—who I'm sure couldn't have told a Boston Red Sox player from a New York Yankee—told my uncomprehending Mum that her doctor wanted to "touch base" with her. A woman in the Isle of Wight Dinosaur Park, sounding like a West Country Carmela Soprano, told her kids that if they wanted to spend some of their pocket money in the shop there then she "would be happy with that". Perhaps the most glaring example during my stay was when a leader of a British Muslim organisation, commenting on the alleged mid-August aeroplane bomb plot, declared, "For me, this is the real deal", presumably stopping himself just in time from adding the word *dude*.

There is something sad, not to mention faintly ridiculous, about all these English people walking about brandishing their national flag while mouthing phrases picked up from TV series filmed in another nation thousands of miles away. Don't get me wrong, I'm not anti-American. I tend, for example, to prefer US writers to English ones. But just because two countries speak the same language doesn't mean they have to speak it the same way. Or, as the English so succinctly put it, we may be in the same ballpark, but that doesn't mean we're on the same page, mate.

Matthew Tree

Peply Conianes

On the Spanish media's persecution
of comedian Pepe Rubianes

Catalonia Today, 25 September 2006

Imagine that the Scottish comedian Billy Connolly decides to write a play about a once-persecuted English writer, let's say Joe Orton, (who the authorities tried to ban for years but who is now very much part of the English literary canon).

Imagine that in an interview about his play on Scottish television, Connolly slags off right-wing England, using the odd F-word. A week later the English media launch an anti-Connolly campaign, reproducing the controversial part of his interview out of context. Connolly apologises many times over for any offence caused.

Eight months later, Connolly's play is scheduled to appear in a London public theatre, the Barbican. Its artistic director is flooded with calls and messages from irate English patriots threatening to murder him if he allows the "traitor" Connolly's play to be performed. Connolly, hearing the fear in the director's voice, decides to back down. On top of everything, both he and the Scottish journalist who interviewed him in January are given a court summons for "injuries to the English nation". The Conservative Party gives its full support to all of this.

Far-fetched? Maybe in the UK, but not in Spain. For Billy Connolly, read Pepe Rubianes (the Galician-born comedian resident in Catalonia) and for Joe Orton, read García Lorca, about whom Rubianes has written a play which will now not be performed in a Madrid public theatre because of a spate of nationalistic death threats. He and his Catalan interviewer Albert Om are awaiting trial on anti-patriotic charges. The Partido Popular are applauding such censorship loudly from the sidelines.

Picasso's daughter famously refused to allow his painting *Guernica* into Spain until it became a democracy, deciding the time was right in 1981. There are moments when it really feels like she jumped the gun.

Lovelace, Linda

On pornography

Catalonia Today, 26 September 2006

When I arrived in Catalonia in the 1980s, I was astonished by the wide variety of hard core pornography available at just about every corner newsstand. (In the UK, it was still illegal to publish an image of an erect penis.)

Only prudes would deny that pornography can be sexually arousing, but I have to admit that whenever I get a peek, I can't help wondering—even as my erection gets under way—just how happy the people in the images are to be there.

This weekend I finally read a book I have long suspected might provide some answers: *Ordeal* by Linda Lovelace, the star of *Deep Throat*, the skin flick that kick-started the mainstream porn industry most of us take for granted today. If *Ordeal* is true, before *Deep Throat*, Lovelace was forced into prostitution by a violent control freak called Chuck Traynor, who also forced her to have sex with a dog, to be anally hemorrhaged by a pathological dominatrix, and to give various mafia and showbiz types her trademark blowjob; he even beat her up on the set of *Deep Throat* (the bruises are clearly visible in certain scenes).

Contrary to the pornographers who rubbished the book for years (as did the makers of the 2005 documentary *Inside Deep Throat*) I for one am convinced that *Ordeal*, recently reprinted, contains not a single fabrication. Linda Lovelace was one miserable woman, and *Deep Throat*, championed by the anti-censorship movement worldwide, was made on the back of years of physical and psychological torture. Not all porn stars have suffered like Lovelace, of course, but her story is a reminder that pornography, like sex itself, is a kind of playing with fire. It can be great fun. Or it can hurt like hell.

Aftertaste

On a controversial speech

Catalonia Today, 2 October 2006

Yet another good *Festa de la Mercè* has gone by, with its fireworks and processions and whatnot. Unfortunately, this year it included two events that left a nasty taste in many Barcelonans' mouths, mine included. The first was the inaugural speech read by the Madrid-based children's author Elvira Lindo. Not because it was in Spanish. Not because Lindo has as much to do with Barcelona as I do with, say, Ulaanbaatar. Not because she couldn't pronounce the great Catalan poet Joan Brossa's name, while claiming to be a close friend of his. Nor because her speech was a rambling, excruciatingly vacuous, cringe-makingly egocentric piece of hogwash. No, what got my goat was the fact that she was only giving this speech in the first place because Joan Clos, Mayor of Barcelona at the time, offered her the job out of the blue when he ran into her at a party in New York last summer. That the traditional start to a festival involving nearly two million people should be spoilt by such an arbitrary, autocratic, and ill-considered choice of speaker was perceived as a right royal insult by plenty of us citizens.

The second event was the *Festa del Cel*, which I took my kids along to, not realising that it consisted of watching Spanish fighter-bombers buzzing the beaches. I tried to make the best of the situation by explaining to the kids that if and when the Catalans unilaterally declare independence, these planes will be back sharpish to nip them in the bud. It struck me that should some form of reprisal be in order afterwards, the Spanish government could do worse than have Elvira Lindo open every single *Festa de la Mercè*, year after year after year, until the Catalans, chastised beyond endurance, abandon all resistance.

Murder Most Foul

On the murder of Anna Politkovskaya

Catalonia Today, 10 October 2006

In Chechnya, since 1991 approximately one hundred thousand people, mainly civilians, have been killed by Russian or Russian-backed security forces, who have also subjected the surviving nine-tenths of the population to rape, torture, kidnappings and other atrocities, including football matches played with human heads and the sale of recently shot Chechens to families that wish to give them an Islamic burial.

These and many other details of life in Chechnya can be found in *A Dirty War* and *A Small Corner Of Hell*, two books available in English and written by Anna Politkovskaya, who for years risked her life to document the Chechen war with a persistence that eventually made her into Russia's most famous journalist.

Politkovskaya, aged 48, was shot dead outside her Moscow flat last Sunday, October 8th, presumably as a gift to Federation president Vladimir Putin, who was celebrating his birthday at the time. With her die the hopes of millions of people that the Russian military—one of the most criminal in the world, say I—might one day be held accountable for their actions. So will there now be demos, protests, and cries of outrage, in Catalonia and elsewhere? Will we be boycotting Russian goods, or standing vigil outside the Russian consulate, or banging our saucepans in the twilight? I doubt it, given that neither the US or Israel are involved, and the excuse for a left wing movement in this country (as deliriously single-minded as it is distressingly non-observant) has been drumming it into our heads for years that these are the only two countries that merit any serious protesting. Rest in peace, Anna. I remember the good talk you gave in Barcelona, a couple of years ago. A pity that tiny auditorium was just half full.

Matthew Tree

Fringe Deficits
On the plight of the Catalan-speaking population in Aragon
Catalonia Today, 17 October 2006

I first got to know Joaquín Arqué in his native Fraga, the capital of what is known as the *Franja* (fringe): the southernmost strip of Aragon in which Catalan is widely spoken.

I met him again last week, at a party outside Candasnos, a village half an hour's drive north of Fraga. I mentioned that they didn't seem to understand Catalan at the local hotel. He looked at me in alarm and explained that Candasnos was the first Spanish-speaking town beyond the Franja and added, "If you speak Catalan to the locals, they'll ignore you completely." Once you're beyond the fringe, he explained, anti-Catalan feelings run high.

Which, he added, is why the Aragonese government refuses to give official status to the Catalan spoken within its borders, which means that it cannot be taught in schools. This, despite the fact that the Franja has the highest percentage of Catalan speakers per capita in Spain. (Joaquín's own grandmother could not even speak Spanish.)

I wonder how a Spanish-speaker, when crossing from Aragon into Catalonia, would react to being *ignored completely* in the first Catalan-speaking town he came across, or if he discovered that Spanish was banned in local schools? I think there would be one humdinger of a scandal. I think we would never hear the end of it.

So the next time the centralist media in Spain denounce the supposed—some would say completely imaginary—persecution of Spanish in Catalonia, as is their wont, please remember the very real plight of Joaquín and his tens of thousands of fellow Catalan-speakers on the Franja, most of them still unable to read and write in their mother tongue. As used to be the case with nearly all Catalan speakers in Spain before 1975. The year Franco died.

Soapbox Blues

On the run-up to the 2006 Catalan elections

Catalonia Today, 24 October 2006

The other morning, local militants of the Catalan Socialist Party (PSC) organised a political rally in my Barcelona neighbourhood, smack in the middle of the unrelenting greyness of the plaça de Fort Pienc (near the Auditori). A couple of cheery-faced women stood next to a helium canister and pumped up condom-pink balloon after condom-pink balloon, each with the PSC logo emblazoned on it, barely able to keep up with the demand from the kids swarming over the square.

On top of this, someone else was handing out toffees—their wrappers also stamped *PSC*—to the same kids, so that the square soon looked like a politically sophisticated children's party.

Around one o'clock, however, some twenty or so adults emerged from the shadows clutching shiny PSC pennants on sticks, and congregated diffidently in front of a makeshift stage, on which a man in a dark suit had started to speechify into a microphone. I caught phrases like "we will reduce the differences between social classes", "there must be housing and education for everyone", and so on, delivered with all the spontaneity of a metro beggar's patter.

This token meeting, with its paltry attendance (and I'm sure it would have been much the same if organised by any other political party) would seem to be symptomatic of a general lack of public interest in the upcoming autonomous elections, caused, perhaps, by the state-sponsored hobbling of the Third Autonomy Statute, which has made it clear to many voters here that the entire Catalan Parliament has less political clout in Madrid than, say, a television chef. Indeed, it wouldn't surprise me if more than a few Catalans now suspect that the old saying according to which voting would be illegal if it could change anything, was invented especially for them.

Just Try It

On John Giorno

Catalonia Today, 30 October 2006

I wasn't as impressed as I'd expected to be when I first saw American poet John Giorno read, in Barcelona's CCCB back in the late 'Nineties. (He did a single whiney poem, going through a succession of coyly camp postures.) After all, this man had been the link between the Beat Generation and Pop Art, had played a vital role on the New York cultural scene for over forty years and had also been a close friend of William Burroughs, whose death he presenced, which for me put Giorno up there with the Apostles (or any other high-ranking acolytes you care to name).

He must have had an off night, because when I met him the next day he proved to be one of the livest of live wires it has ever been my luck to listen to. He talked about Warhol and Rauschenberg—ex-lovers both—and the attitude that he and they had had in their heyday: "Don't worry about whether an idea is good or bad, just try it and see if it works," he said, making me feel better about my writing than I had done in a long time.

We finished up in the Corte Inglés, as John needed cigarette papers for joints. I got a quiet kick out of the sales assistant's disapproving glare when John ordered several packs of king-size Rizlas. Had he known of Giorno's violent, chillingly repetitive poems, or his prose accounts of wild toilet sex with Keith Haring et al, I dare say that glare would have blasted us right across the Plaça de Catalunya. Such poetry and prose, I discovered recently, can be found in John's only book still in print, *You Got To Burn To Shine* (1994). As the slogan goes: hurry now, while stocks last.

Bunch of C's

On a new political party

Catalonia Today, 7 November 2006

A new coalition party (*Ciutadans-Partido de la Ciudadania*, usually abbreviated as *C's*) has won three seats in the Catalan parliament. Its members claim that they recognise no national community whatsoever—their avowed "non-nationalism' can, logically, mean nothing else—which would make them practically unique among human beings, were it true. But their manifesto reveals that their main concern is with nothing other than an apparently excessive use of the Catalan language in Catalonia. Unfortunately, that isn't all.

My first indication of this came from a friend who helped found the party (name withheld, given that Ciutadans has a habit of publicly slandering anyone that falls foul of it). He left after six months, when he noticed that more than a few sympathisers were turning up at party rallies with Spanish-flag badges pinned to their lapels (a sure sign of far rightness). It is surely no coincidence, then, that of the two Ciutadans voters I know of, one finds the ultraconservative Partido Popular too moderate, and the other used to support the Falange. Neither can it be a coincidence that Ciutadans has received the blessing of Esteban Gómez-Rovira, the founder of a neo-fascist party called Juntas Españolas. However, it should be pointed out that Ciutadans also has some left-wing voters, who, astonishingly, don't mind being bedfellows with people who still have wet dreams about Franco. It would seem that a common antipathy towards a Catalanish Catalonia (as opposed to a wholly Hispanified one) has brought certain lefties and fascisti together, with the result that the voice of the extreme Spanish nationalist right has finally managed to sneak into the Catalan parliament though a back door opened by a "non-nationalist" party. Citizens, my arse.

Matthew Tree

Something New
On Africa
Catalonia Today, 13 November 2006

The other week, after a talk in a school in Mataró, I got chatting to Alioune Sangaré, a 17 year old student of African origin. His Catalan was so good I assumed that he was Catalan himself (eg, born here). No, no, he corrected me, he only arrived two years ago. Two years ago! I squawked, before asking where he was from. He told me French Guinea. So, in a mere two years, starting at age 15, this young man had learnt to speak, write, and read both Catalan and Spanish from scratch. For my part, I didn't even know the name of his country's capital city.

Indeed, I have long suffered from a flabbergasting ignorance of all things African. Soon after meeting Alioune in Mataró, however, I started reading everything I could lay my hands on about the continent. Since then, I have been astonished to find that Botswana is its most politically and economically successful country in per capita terms; that Equatorial Guinea was turned into a hell of rape, pillage, and murder by Franco's pathological placeman, Macías Nguema, and that Somalia had once been a stable, culturally and linguistically unified country, before being chopped into its current unworkable enclaves by five different colonial powers; or that the entire continent had once been a shifting, dynamic network of politically heterogenous cultures, ranging from authoritarian empires to what would now be called anarchist communities. I even found out that the capital of Alioune's native country is Conakry. Every fresh fact has been a minor revelation, obliterating the hackneyed clichés I'd had about Africa for so long. Finally, I was able to appreciate the truth of Pliny the Elder's famous phrase: "Out of Africa, always something new." Fortunately for us, some of this something—and Alioune Sangaré is just one fine example—has come to Catalonia.

Bane of Our Lives

On the inefficiency of Spanish ISPs

Catalonia Today, 20 November 2006

Last Thursday I was on the evening train from Girona as it crept towards Barcelona at its usual leisurely pace. People were reading or dozing in a silence broken only by the gentle jiggering of the bogies. All of a sudden, the entire carriage was startled out of its wits by a voice screaming "CONY DE TELÈFON! T'HE DIT 'OTROS SERVICIOS', COLLONS! ETS SORD O QUÈ?!" (*"Damn telephone! I said 'other services'! Are you deaf?!"*) I looked up to find a plump man in his thirties glaring with undisguised hatred at a cellphone clutched furiously in his chubby paw. I guessed that when trying to solve some telecommunications-related problem he had come up against the usual impenetrable barrier of recorded help messages.

My heart went out to him. After all, barely a soul in this country has been spared the incoherent technical support, the infuriating inefficiency and the insufferable arrogance of the phone companies and ISPs which have wheedled themselves into our lives and now feed off us on a monthly basis. In the space of three years, for instance, I have had to deal with dozens of mysteriously vanishing emails (Wanadoo), technicians who only knew how to configure two Microsoft programmes, neither of which I had (Telefonica), and a cellphone company (Amena, which recently turned Orange) that repeatedly cut me off when abroad and then lost my phone when I handed it in for repairs nearly a year ago.

In a nutshell, the most sophisticated communications technology yet known to mankind seems to be in the hands of a handful of bumbling money-grubbers who wouldn't know a USB socket from a WAP browser. If God were to sort this gormless lot out once and for all, why, I do declare I'd start believing in Him.

Fifteen Minutes
On fame
Catalonia Today, 28 November 2006

If you decide to make a writer of yourself, the chances are your family will suspect you are not only hopelessly unrealistic but deluded to boot, and your friends will look on you with the pity they normally reserve for sect victims. Nobody, in fact, will believe you really are a writer except you, until you manage to publish something.

In my case, this took some fifteen years. So when my first novel finally came out, in 1996, I was determined that it would not be drowned, kitten-fashion, in that whirlpool of disinterest which ensnares so many novice authors. To this end, I desperately scrounged whatever interviews I could get from the media. It seemed to work, in the sense that not only was there a second edition, but I also managed to establish myself as a small but visible hamlet on the Catalan literary map.

Thereafter, I continued to court the broadcasters until it dawned on me that something was going very wrong. The strangers who occasionally greeted me on the street made it clear they had seen my head talking on the telly, but hadn't so much as glimpsed my name in print. In short, my modicum of fame, far from helping to establish my credentials as a writer, had turned me into a minor local figurine and little more. Therefore it was a pleasant shock when, last Saturday, someone introduced herself as a reader of mine. Indeed, I was so surprised I couldn't utter a word of the gratitude that was bubbling up inside me. So: if she happens to read this and sends me a postal address, I'd be more than happy to defy the usual Spanish boycott and send her a bottle of cava, by way of a belated but genuine thank-you.

A Prick in Time Saves Nine

On Catalan-hating English residents
in Catalonia

Catalonia Today, 5 December 2006

On the website *barcelonareporter.com*, a Scotsman called Nick recently criticised an English barman in Barcelona who knows Catalan but insists on speaking to local customers in Spanish because, as this barman so robustly puts it, "It really pisses the little Catalan pricks off." Nick bemoans the fact that this kind of attitude (reminiscent, I would add, of that of Franco's functionaries in their heyday or—if the word *kaffir* is substituted for *Catalan*—of those chinless officials who made the British Empire what it used to be) is widespread within the more endogamic sector of Catalonia's *guiri* (foreign) community.

That won't come as a surprise to anyone who has ever dipped so much as a toe into that chilly social pond. What is notable, however, is that the only British critic of such racism on *barcelonareporter.com* should be, precisely, a Scot. Scotland has long been a country both canny and surprising and, if all goes well, will soon be springing the biggest surprise of all—political independence, which 52% of Scots now want, according to recent surveys—on a European Union whose most revered ideal, to judge by its actions, is the preservation of the borders of existing sovereign states.

If and when the Scots secede, it will only be a matter of time before the Catalans also manage to free themselves up. Meanwhile, perhaps Nick would be so kind as to send me the name and address of the bar tended by his rancourous English expat. Myself and many other little Catalan-speaking pricks (including certain Italian, Dutch, Moroccan and Peruvian friends of mine) would just love to celebrate Independence Day there, together with its friendly staff. I'm assuming drinks will be on the house.

Matthew Tree

Jungle Jinx
On being legal
Catalonia Today, 12 December 2006

Last week I met councillor Xavier Trias (Convergència i Unió's candidate for Mayor of Barcelona) on Xavier Graset's political chat show, *L'Oracle*, on Catalunya Ràdio, and please forgive all this wanton name dropping.

We kicked off with a discussion about Barcelona's squatters. Trias revealed himself to be that most predictable of opinionators: a died-in-the-wool legalist. Squatting contravened the law, he said, and so should be dealt with immediately by the police. Not to respect the letter of the law, he added, would be tantamount to "living in the jungle". He remained unmoved by factors such as the current desperate housing shortage, or the extremely positive achievements of some squatting collectives: if they were illegal, out they would go (just, indeed, as they have always had to go, ever since squatting started in Barcelona).

That same day, another convinced legalist, Catalonia's socialist president José Montilla, ordered his ministers to respect the small print of the Constitution by flying both the Spanish and Catalan flags from public buildings (and not, for example, the Catalan flag alone). Interestingly, he omitted to impose this same two-flags law on any of the public buildings controlled by the Policía Nacional and the Spanish military, which have forever only flown the flag of the Spanish state. Highly illicit. What is more, Mr Trias, his apparent terror of jungle life notwithstanding, hasn't so much as whispered one word of complaint about this flagrant flouting of the legal code. Perhaps because he knows in his heart of hearts that an unacknowledged but important aspect of the law is that those who break it with impunity, do so in order to make it clear who's really boss.

We Know It's Christmas

On Christmas 2006

Catalonia Today, 19 December 2006

One of the best things about Christmas, says I, is that it has all but lost its religious significance. I can still remember when the high point of the Xmas Season was Midnight Mass, but all that wafer swallowing and wine tasting and traipsing round the neighbourhood behind a man dressed as a 14th century Byzantine businessman is now merely a faint and uncherished memory. These days, Christmas revolves, thankfully, around two activities as worldly as they are worthwhile: giving and getting gifts and bolting fancy foods. Even here in Catalonia, where so many kids set up nativity scenes in the living-room, any religious overtones are neatly undercut by the placing of a little man dropping a sizeable log within spitting distance of the King of Kings.

Christmas is now, says I, the best break of the year, when, for once, there is nothing for it but to hunker down in the warm and forget the world's evil and chaos even as it shifts and stirs in exotic places. Christmas, in other words, is a time to be as cosy and irresponsible as a child, as the children now giggling and howling with excitement in every nook and cranny at the thought of Christmas which they know full well is nothing to do with any supposed God on Earth, but rather with playing and pleasure, a playing and pleasure they will surely recall as adults—as I do now—when they will try and recapture some of that unfettered, unqualified yuletide happiness by diving into the cubby hole of Christmas Time with a bottle in one hand and a full glass in the other, from which they will take sip after redeeming sip before dozing off in front of Charlton Heston pretending to be Moses.

Missionary Position
On a great African novel

Catalonia Today, 15 January 2007

At one of those deliciously boozy meals that follow one another in sluggish succession through the twelve days of Christmas, I got talking to author and anthropologist Albert Sánchez Piñol about Africa, which he has been visiting for near on two decades. According to him, it's the missionaries who are the worst of the white blights: "For every thirty languages they take away, they give back one," he raged, "while criminalising local religions and then fobbing the natives off with a kiddies' version of Christianity," thus causing untold harm to hundreds of complex cultures.

By coincidence, that week I had stumbled across a recently reprinted autobiographical novel which dealt with precisely this subject. In Tsitsi Dangarembga's *Nervous Conditions* (1988), a village girl in Ian Smith's Rhodesia describes how she goes to Mission School and makes friends there with the black headmaster's daughter, an anglicised (and anorexic) teenager who has seen through the colonisers' paternalistic game and hates what they have made her into, yet can't be anything else. This friend ends up having a terrifying fit, consumed by fury against both herself and her educators. For this reader at least, Dangarembga's novel, beautifully written, with plenty of subtle jabs at the white solar plexus, also carries the revelatory thrill of hearing an entire continent whisper to itself about the cultural culdesac into which it has been jammed by alien hands.

So how is it that, far from granting this fine novel modern classic status, most European readers haven't even heard of it? Surely, Europeans today don't have that inbuilt condescension towards African culture that was and is so rife among the missionaries? In my mind's ear, I can hear Sánchez Piñol— no fool he—chuckling cynically in the background.

Bull from the Beeb

On the BBC's misrepresentation of the Catalans

Catalonia Today, 16 January 2007

On the 4th of this month, one Marian Hens broadcast a programme about immigration in Catalonia on the BBC's Radio Four which—conditioned by the breathtakingly superficial research that tends to characterise English media reports on the area—presented the Catalans as "fiercely nationalist" ethnocentric xenophobes hell-bent on forcing their "local language" (sic) down the throats of helpless foreign residents.

I am not suggesting that English journalists have to assume—as died-in-the-wool zealots like myself do—that Catalonia is no more Spain than Scotland is England and that political independence would be a blessing for everyone both inside and outside Catalonia, but it would be nice not to have everything remotely pro-Catalan branded as selfish and racist, *a priori*. Ms Hens could easily have counterbalanced her one-sided portrait of this complicated corner of Europe by mentioning, say, the Linguistic Volunteer programmes for recently arrived adults, a pioneering and highly successful initiative that plenty of nations would surely copy, if only someone—a BBC reporter, for example—took the trouble to tell them about it. Had she bothered to visit any of the adult education centres around the country she would have found surprisingly large numbers of Catalonia's million or so newcomers taking a considerable personal interest in the "local language", which many of them, like I myself, didn't know existed before they arrived. Perhaps because they have cottoned on to the fact that many (sadly not all) Catalans consider this language to be a kind of natural, easily accessible passport to their country, far more important than blood—a meaningless race-based concept which most European states nonetheless still use as a key factor when granting nationality. Britain included. Please, Ms Hens, Ms Hens, please: kindly remove that beam from your eye.

Matthew Tree

Son of a Bitch
On swearing
Catalonia Today, 22 January 2007

A month or so ago, as I was boring the pants off a small group of secondary school students on the Maresme coast with a talk about some dull language-related subject, it occurred to me, in my plodding old-man way, to liven things up for my captive audience by asking them about bilingual insults: was an *hijo de puta*, for example, worse than a *fill de puta* or the other way round? Almost everyone thought that an insult in Spanish sounded harder than one in Catalan. This was confirmed with knobs on by those who had seen Tarantino's expletive-stuffed *Pulp Fiction* in both Catalan and Spanish: his supposedly foul-mouthed gangsters just didn't ring true when using the vernacular of Jacint Verdaguer.

A pity that back then I couldn't have surprised and perhaps even pleasantly shocked those students with a taste of the finest Catalan cursing I have ever come across, published just a week ago in *Missa Pagesa [Peasant Mass]* by Dolors Miquel, whose public readings, in which she belts out what many people consider to be some of the best contemporary poetry in Catalan to the sound of music, never fail to bring the house down. In this new book, Miquel has assembled a formidable hoard of curses from her native Lleida and squeezed them into prayer form, as in her blasphemous feminist version of the Lord's Prayer: "Our Mother who is in rut/hallowed be thy cunt." Where she really lets her hair down, though, is in her "homilies" to certain types of modern fool (get the book for more details): "filthy goatlets, arse-licking twats who swallow it all/crumb-scrounging dogs, lickers of power-brokers/sitting there in the stalls for the tight-arsed/dunking bank-notes in your shitholes." Quentin Tarantino, eat your heart out.

Let There Be Light

On alternative science

Catalonia Today, 29 January 2007

In last week's issue of *El Temps* magazine, the Valencian philosopher, historian, novelist and translator of Dante, Joan Francesc Mira, expressed his flabbergastedness at the fact that in France, the very country which had ushered in the Enlightenment, the industries generated by what is now called "alternative science" shifted a mind-numbing 4,500 million euros in 2006.

His surprise surprised me. Ever since the 1970s, huge numbers of apparently rational Europeans—who know, for example, that the little person reading the television news doesn't actually live in the set—have sworn to the efficacy of aromatherapy, numerology and other such wistful beliefs, not to mention that most respectable of quack scams, homeopathy.

The Catalans, of course, are no exception. There is barely a town in the country which doesn't boast a shop that deals in toy pyramids, magnetic bangles and a host of books on every non-existent subject under the sun, from Neo-Theosophy to the Blank Rune Controversy.

I, too, used to swallow such pigswill. Hey, I was young. I longed to know more than was good for me about my health, my love life, and in which decade I might publish my first book, so I turned to the army of charlatans that was itching to help. This meant that for a while I seriously believed that real effects could have seemingly impossible causes. It was only later I realised that once you throw common sense out of the window, you can end up believing all kinds of dangerous garbage. Many of the neo-Nazis who are on the ascendant everywhere in Europe are also vocal defenders of "alternative science"; taking their cue, I suppose, from their beloved Hitler, who, before setting in motion the murder of millions, checked with his astrologist first.

Matthew Tree

Nip and Tuck

On Japanese and not-so-Japanese restaurants in Barcelona

Catalonia Today, 5 February 2007

About twenty years ago, Japanese restaurants in Barcelona were like those in any other major European city: thin on the ground and sky-high in price. I remember envying bankers, private dentists, property speculators and other objectively unlikeable professionals their access to establishments like the Yashima (still there on Avinguda Tarradellas) where they could gorge themselves on foods as mysterious as they were unobtainable.

About ten years ago, however, Japanese restaurants suddenly got so fashionable they almost became as two-a-penny as their ubiquitous Chinese counterparts. Not long after, what's more, a third wave of more modest-looking Japanese restaurants swept in, characterised by remarkably, even suspiciously low prices. Attracted by what looked like a bargain, when one opened near me I gave it a try.

The decoration was certainly Japanese, right down to a sushi conveyor belt. It wasn't until I took a closer look at the staff, however, chefs included, that I realised they were all as Chinese as Won-Ton soup, despite their kanji-covered uniforms. The owner had clearly decided to cash in on the fad for "Japos", assuming that all us Westerners were fools who couldn't tell one slanty-eyed nation (as the Duke of Edinburgh might have put it) from another. Perhaps he had a point: to this day, enough Catalans are still being conned by these ersatz-Japanese restaurants—that serve thinly disguised Cantonese dishes together with the odd bit of raw fish—to make them going concerns.

Since then I have managed to find just one restaurant in Barcelona that is both genuinely Japanese and reasonably priced: the Hana Bishi, on Balmes 55. It has a friendly multilingual staff and great sushi and three brands of Japanese beer to choose from. And no belts attached.

Just Couldn't Cope

On a hatemongering radio station

Catalonia Today, 15 February 2007

I have friends who've done it. The novelist Rosa Regàs even wrote an article in *El País* about doing it. Last Friday, for the first time in my life, I did it. I leaned forward in the taxi and told the driver to either switch off the radio or let me out. Like my friends, like Rosa Regàs, I had suffered a surprise attack of disgust, courtesy of the COPE, the bishop-backed, righter-than-right, ultra-patriotic radio station.

What made me snap up in my seat was a "COPE special report" about ETA member De Juana Chaos, who is on hunger strike in a Madrid prison, in protest, at the time, at being given an extra 12 years for writing two allegedly pro-terrorist newspaper articles, just when he was due to be released after completing an 18 year sentence for murder. Recent photos show a skeleton draped in flesh which, doctors say, could die any day now.

Not according to the COPE, though, which claimed that De Juana Chaos was nothing but a cynical showman who was taking the mickey out of the honest Spanish public by secretly living the life of Riley, with "all kinds of very special privileges". I suddenly realised that millions of listeners were being psychologically groomed to welcome, even to desire, the judiciary-sponsored euthanasia of a Basque prisoner. This sort of low-intensity hate-mongering, what's more, will as good as ensure that De Juana's death will set off an unprecedented spate of political slander, street violence, gerrymandered trials and general overall nastiness in both Euskadi and Spain.

The COPE having been momentarily silenced and my destination reached, I politely thanked the driver for the journey, and he politely thanked me for the tip. In Catalonia, at least, we are all still pretending to be nice to each other.

Carnival Schmarnival

On the inconvenience of Carnival

Catalonia Today, 22 February 2007

Many, many moons ago, all over the world people used to fret forever about whether their sheep would lamb and their cattle calve and their corn grow high before the harvest time. So every year, by way of a spiritual guarantee, they raised one of their young men to the status of a fertility god and worshipped him until the following Spring. Then they killed him and put another man, even younger and more strapping, in his place, believing his fresh vigour would continue to guarantee them meat and cereals in abundance. Later, it occurred to these mortal gods to have their sons conveniently sacrificed in their place (echoes of this practice can be found in the story of Abraham and Isaac). Later still, it was decided to make a condemned criminal into the god, given that he was due to be lapidated—or crucified—anyway. Before his execution, the local population fornicated to its heart's content, in a magical attempt to stimulate the growth of the crop and the tupping of the livestock.

Over the centuries, this ancient ritual involving group sex and human sacrifice was slowly mitigated into today's Carnival. I mention this in the hope that primary school teachers around Catalonia will come to the conclusion that this festival is really not at all suitable for young children, which would mean that me and my girlfriend would then not have to spend three bloody nights in a row sewing bits of coloured cloth onto our kids' clothes only to realise we've botched the job and then have to rush out at the last minute to purchase two ridiculously over-priced fancy dress outfits, every sodding February. And not a Bacchanalia in sight to make up for the inconvenience.

The Exit Sign

On how much bullshit the Catalans seem to be prepared to take

Catalonia Today, 2 March 2007

By the time Franco finally expired, the Catalans were pretty much disliked and distrusted in the rest of Spain—I remember one army officer suggesting on the radio circa 1978 that most of them should be put in concentration camps—but they assumed that with time, once Spaniards had learnt that Catalonia had a different culture, history and social structure, all inherited from an independent past, they would also understand that she needed enough leeway to find her own solutions to her problems—both linguistic and economic—many of which had been caused, indeed, by Franco's pathologically centralist and uniformist regime.

Thirty years on, it is obvious to all but the wilfully cloistered that most Castilianist Spaniards not only have learnt nothing about Catalonia, but that their dislike, in many cases, has morphed into a kind of simmering loathing. For instance, speaking Catalan in monolingual Spain is now something of a high-risk sport, unless you happen to be as quick-witted as satirical writer Empar Moliner, who, on being bawled at by her Madrid taxi driver that she should stop speaking Catalan on her mobile, promptly lied that she was talking in Italian. "Entonces," the driver said, in all seriousness, "no pasa nada."

Such prejudice means that any pro-Catalan policy is a natural vote-loser, which is probably why the Constitutional Tribunal was recently rigged to block the new Catalan Statute of Autonomy, at the same time as an almost identical Andalusian Statute is being passed with barely a hiccup.

Personally, if I find myself in a room full of people who I know don't like me, I walk out. The Catalans, for reasons that I am unable to fathom, are dithering by the door, wondering what they can still do to get in everyone's good graces. Pathetic, or what?

Strangling Animals
Is Just Fine

On TV censorship and Michael Palin's diaries

Catalonia Today, 8 March 2007

For Christmas, I was given the diaries of Michael Palin, a key member of *Monty Python's Flying Circus*, the 1970s BBC comedy series whose influence has extended all over the world in the course of the last thirty years (Catalonia included, as watchers of TV3's *Polònia* well know). However, anyone hoping to discover the creative processes that led to internationally imitated sketches such as "The Cheese Shop" or the liberating blockbuster *The Life of Brian*, will not get so much as a jot of insight from Palin's 600 pages. Ranging in scope from the commonplace to the mundane, Palin spills not a single bean: the weather, his meals, superficially described script meetings, and his idyllically static private life make up the bulk of the book.

Just one revelation lurks amidst all this surface detail: the astonishing degree of censorship exercised by UK and US television at the time. For example, in a Python parody of a quiz show, one of the contestants had his hobbies listed as "golf, strangling animals and masturbating". The BBC vetoed the most universal of these three pastimes. On another occasion, the BBC green-lighted one "piss off" but warned that two would be "excessive".

The Americans were stricter to the point of parody: ABC, for example, removed the word "bitch" when referring to a dog.

Such censorship, of course, is still with us—for proof, we need look no further than Spanish and Catalan television—waging war on anything that both shocks and delights: "anything to do with life" as comic author Douglas Adams put it. So I have no qualms in using this modest platform of a column to tell TV censors everywhere, once and for all, that they should quite simply piss off. Twice, if necessary.

Publishers Be Damned

On getting rejected by a UK publisher

Catalonia Today, 15 March 2007

In the years before I staggered, as nervous as I was legless, onto the train out of Victoria Station that eventually took me to twenty-two years in Catalonia, I hadn't had much luck with publishers. I would send them my work and they would send me back depressingly impersonal rejection slips of the "not-right-for-us-good-luck-elsewhere' type. It was like being given the big E week after week from a self-satisfied doorman guarding a club to which he had no intention of admitting me. Ever.

So, when my first book was finally published (in Barcelona and in Catalan), in what must be a record-breaking fit of pique I made up my mind to publish only in Catalonia and not to send any more material to Britain. Ever.

One month ago, though, given that I had recently completed a full-length book in English, I finally decided to break my own rule and sent it off to a London publisher. Last Tuesday, he sent me back a depressingly imper-sonal rejection slip of the "not-right-for-us-good-luck-elsewhere" type. For a moment, I was in front of that po-faced doorman again, getting my umpteenth E. Except that this time round I have enough published books under my belt to know that publishers are far more like waiters than door-men: writers cook up the goods and paying customers enjoy them, *chacun à son goût*. Publishers are nothing but clumsy go-betweens, who are forever slipping up and sending the dishes crashing to the floor. Far from feeling piqued, I have now resigned myself to the fact that, in Britain at least, I have no choice but to simply keep on handing these flunkeys my plate until one of them manages to get it to the right table.

Blighty

On getting very nervous about going to London

Catalonia Today, 22 March 2007

I have just woken up at half past five in the morning, and know I will never get back to sleep, on the *qui vive* as I now am for impending disasters. My heart rate has accelerated and my self-esteem has shrunk, pardon the image, like a penis in a springtime sea. And all this simply because I will soon be on a plane to London.

Why, I ask myself, wide-eyed and yearning for a tranquillising Lorezepam, does the thought of visiting the city where I was born and brought up always shake me up so?

All right, I'll tell me. Ever since I decided to stop living there, London has been the psychological equivalent of a cured tumour (not the people I know there, just the place itself). To walk its streets is to remind myself that I had to leave them, way back when, because I became convinced that otherwise I would end up an alcoholic or a funny farm resident or, quite possibly, both. Indeed, I still suspect that had I stayed in London—which I have long thought of as a callous, even merciless city—I would not have made it to my current age or, if I had, I would be wishing I hadn't.

Which is why I find it particularly irritating when I run into one of those Catalans—and there are a few—who insist on cooing about how wonderful my home city is, especially by way of contrast to "provincial" Barcelona. I refrain from asking these aspiring Citizens-Of-The-World why they don't go and live there themselves if they like it so much, and take a certain silent pleasure in imagining them trying to do so. It's as good a revenge as any other.

Gat Flap

On the bizarre security measures
at Gatwick Airport

Catalonia Today, 29 March 2007

Leaving the UK via Gatwick Airport these days—last Monday, in my case—is proof positive that religion-inspired terrorism has put the fear of God into those responsible for ensuring security. Once I'd checked in, I was placed in a dense departure queue which wasn't moving an inch, making it impossible to get away from a hovering bevy of twenty year olds in yellow T-shirts who were jiggling little plastic bags in the air while bawling "creams!, pastes!, necessary liquids!" into the patient ears of the queuers. This racket was only interrupted by the PA system, which informed us every two minutes in a voice oozing cold control that if we left any bags unattended, they would be destroyed immediately. No sooner had I been told by another passenger that the reason for the delay was a fire alarm, than I was pushed out of the way by an officious-looking old codger muttering into a walkie-talkie attached to a fluorescent sou'wester, his eyes fixed on a distant and presumably risk-laden spot.

An hour later, the flap resolved itself and I finally made it into the duty-free area from which I dashed to the departure gate where, puffing and panting, I ran by coincidence into Stephen Burgen, novelist and contributing editor to this magazine. He listened feelingly to how my nerves had been frazzled to a crisp by all this security kerfuffle, and, by way of consolation, assured me that Heathrow was "even worse". Although we were talking in English, a Catalan sentence suddenly popped into my head: *em cago en Déu*. Highly appropriate, now I think about it.

Matthew Tree

A Wing and a Prayer

On the infeasibility of monotheism

Catalonia Today, 5 April 2007

A flame of controversy has leapt up on the normally placid letters page of the UK's *Times Literary Supplement*. The letters in question concern the best-selling essay *The God Delusion*, by the English scientist Richard Dawkins, in which the author affirms that science and religion are incompatible, that religions are negative and superfluous side effects of evolutionary development, and that the world would be a safer and freer place if a majority of its population were humanist atheists.

Especially interesting about the controversy is the tone of the letters from the pro-religious correspondents. Try as they might to be as clinical and common-sensical as their pro-science adversaries, a hysterical, outraged note always manages to creep in at some point in their arguments. In a nut-shell, they do protest too much.

This, I may say, has generally been my experience with religious people: in the end, they treat any negation of their beliefs as a deeply felt insult, thus creating an atmosphere of untouchability around spiritual credos in general, to the extent that anyone who publicly states that virgin births or virgin-populated paradises, say, are nothing more than desperately fanciful products of the imagination, is immediately subject to any amount of holy vitriol. As was William Burroughs (1914-1997), when he launched his definitive attack on theism in general: "Consider the impasse of a one-God universe: He is all knowing and all powerful. He can't go anywhere since he is already every-where. He can't do anything since the act of doing presupposes opposition. His universe is irrevocably thermodynamic, having no friction by definition. So He has to create friction—War! Fear! Sickness! Death!—just to keep His dying show on the road..." Please think about it, all you devout monotheists out there, before you reach for your outrage.

The Rain in Spain

On a bit of police torture being revealed
in the Press

Catalonia Today, 13 April 2007

Last Good Friday, Barcelona's *Avui* newspaper confirmed the Basque government had evidence that ten people arrested by the Guardia Civil on March 28th under suspicion of being members of ETA, had been tortured in various Madrid police stations. One of their lawyers has stated specifically that for five days his client was beaten on the back, face, and testicles, and repeatedly reduced to near suffocation by having a plastic bag tied over his head.

That the Guardia Civil torture detainees is no more newsworthy than that the Pope prays on Sundays. The real news is the news item itself. For decades, the Spanish police have kept the media off their backs by firmly denying charges of torture, sometimes even as their battered victims are being wheeled out of the back door. The public at large, for instance, never found out for 23 years about the treatment meted out to university professor Carles Castellanos when he was arrested in 1988, suspected (wrongly) of being a member of the armed Catalan group *Terra Lliure*. He was blindfolded, bound hand and foot, beaten frequently, and subjected to phony executions and other threats. (He especially remembers the guards' promise to "gang-fuck your Catalan whore of a wife".) We wouldn't know about this ordeal even now, had he not published his memoirs in 2003.

Indeed, so little attention do the media give police torture, they would appear to take it quite for granted, like the rain in May. Myself, whenever I read the current reports about the political ups and downs of the Basque peace process, I cannot help but hear, in the background, a frantic wheezing behind plastic: a cellar echo that gives the lie to the righteous proclamations of the talking heads we know so well.

Matthew Tree

Round the Table
On the unwitting arrogance
of an international expert
Catalonia Today, 19 April 2007

When I first came to Barcelona I was rude, shockingly rude, day in and night out. I know this because I was told as much by English people who judged my speaking to Catalan friends in Catalan, in front of the self-same English people, very poor etiquette indeed. The reason? Yes, you've already guessed. These English people hadn't learnt Catalan and wanted all of us to switch to Spanish, which they had.

I refused, saying that I expressed myself (much) better in Catalan than in Spanish, and that anyway both I and my Catalan friends would have found it deadeningly artificial to change to a language we normally never spoke together (so much so that, even when we tried, we soon lapsed back into Catalan).

This kind of day-to-day linguistic persistence, indeed, is one of the reasons why Catalan has survived three hundred years of attempts to suffocate it into an all but inaudible gasp.

A fact which has not, apparently, made a single blip on the cultural radar of Fred Halliday, a "specialist in international relations"—and part-time Barcelona resident—interviewed in this paper last week. Mr Halliday was most upset about the roundtable discussions he'd attended (in Catalonia) at which Catalan was used with no allowance made for the fact that he didn't understand it. According to him, this was "plain rude".

This reminded me of 20 years ago, when, as I said, I saw many an English *bwana* deigning to break bread with the natives without having bothered to inform himself of their linguistic customs, and then blaming them for being incomprehensible. What astonishingly insufferable haughtiness. And even more so, coming from a specialist in international relations. Where was he working before he came here to tell us how to behave? Iraq?

Freefall

On the outstanding disaster the Catalan section of the RENFE train network has become

Catalonia Today, 26 April 2007

Back in the eighties, using the Catalan segment of the RENFE was a risky business best suited to the young and the wild at heart. Often packed tighter than Q-tips on trains that left with the punctuality of functioning alcoholics, passengers might find themselves suddenly stranded on a remote segment of track for hours on end.

The nineties saw a noticeable improvement, with timetables actually being read by the employees, and new, more spacious rolling stock which made it possible to breathe without bothering the other travellers.

Those golden years, however, are now a thing of the past. In the last seven months, a million and a half Catalan passengers have been truly shafted by 110 separate breakdowns, mainly due to lack of maintenance due in turn, to chronic, and seemingly discriminatory, underfunding. The media here have raised the roof.

So when I took the Girona train last Saturday and arrived two hours late, after an unannounced change in Granollers, a 45 minute wait in Sant Celoni and a 30 minute wait in Riells, I thought I would at least have the satisfaction of reading about it in next day's paper. Not so. My piddling little delay had been trumped by a four hour blockage of the Maresme line (by an empty train) that same morning.

The day before, the Generalitat's negotiators in Madrid had asked to have the Catalan RENFE transferred to them. Affronted, central government rep Víctor Morlans asked them why they thought a Generalitat-controlled network would provide a better service? Sadly, the Catalan negotiators—impeded, no doubt, by their notorious timidity—refrained from giving Sr. Morlans the answer he deserved: that it would be impossible to provide, or even imagine, a worse one.

Butchering the Idiot

A review of: *Murder in Amsterdam - The Death of
Theo van Gogh and the Limits of Tolerance*

Catalonia Today, 28 April 2007

On November 2nd, 2004, Theo van Gogh—a Dutch film-maker and
writer—was cycling home in Amsterdam. When passing through a particularly dreary stretch of street (I was shown the spot last year), he was shot
in the stomach by Mohammed Bouyeri, a twenty-six year old Dutchman
of Moroccan extraction. Van Gogh crawled over to the opposite pavement,
followed by Bouyeri, who, ignoring Van Gogh's shouts of "Don't do it!",
shot him several more times. Bouyeri took out a machete and slashed the
film-maker's throat, then scribbled something on a piece of paper which he
laid on Van Gogh's chest, stabbing it into place with another, smaller, knife.

He was reloading his pistol when the police turned up. As he stated later
in court, his intentions had been to die as a martyr to his "faith" in a shoot-
out. But he got shot in the leg instead, and was taken into custody.

Ian Buruma, a Dutch-born journalist now working in the US, has produced a neatly researched book that puts paid to the media-sponsored clichés—of the "clash-of-cultures" sort—that have hounded this particularly
brutal murder. He points out that Theo van Gogh—although notorious for
his deliberately tasteless attacks against Islam and other religions—enjoyed
working with immigrants as a director and did a bunch of drama series about
the problems facing them in Europe. He even got two Moroccan-Dutch
delinquents out of reform school and helped them become the successful
actors they still are today.

It was perhaps inevitable, then, that he would end up working with
Holland's most high-profile immigrant, the Muslim apostate Ayaan Hirsi
Ali, a Somali refugee who has become famous worldwide as a critic of what
she sees as the appalling misogyny built into conventional Islam. Van Gogh
and Hirsi Ali ended up making a ten minute short *(Submission)* in which texts
from the Koran advocating violence against women are superimposed on
several battered wives in see-through burqas. Designed to provoke debate
in the Dutch Muslim community, *Submission* became the start of Hirsi Ali's

life under armed guard. The note pinned to Van Gogh's chest stated that the director had been killed for directing the film and that Hirsi Ali was next on the list.

As for Bouyeri, far from being a budding religious fanatic, he had been successful and popular at school, and had restricted his religious practices to fasting at Ramadan and little else. However, as he grew older, something changed. An apparent inability to cope with the hedonism of Dutch life, exacerbated by increasing confusion about the sexual rejection he was getting from some women—which he interpreted as racism—led him to shun the folksy Islam of his village-born father and surf the numerous websites of extreme Jihadist theorists, whose ideas are based mainly on those of Ussama bin Laden's intellectual mentor Sayyid Qutb (1906-1966), a viciously misogynist anti-semite who advocated that not only infidels but also non-observant Muslims may be legitimately assassinated. Very soon, Bouyeri was spending his leisure time watching real-life videos of western hostages being tortured and beheaded. The "faith" he later told the court he was defending, had become little more than a whacko Death Cult.

When *Submission* was made, Hirsi Ali begged Van Gogh to take his name off the credits, for safety's sake (as had been done with the crew and actresses). He refused, saying that he was just a "village idiot", a harmless joker, and that no one in his right mind would want to do him in.

Well, Mohammed Bouyeri didn't get the joke and was so far out of his right mind on November 2nd, 2004, that it remains highly unlikely he will ever get any kind of joke, ever again, throughout the term of his long prison life.

Murder in Amsterdam is by Ian Buruma. Atlantic Books, London, 2006. 262 pages.

Matthew Tree

Steal This Newspaper

On a not unclever teenage rebel in Sant Cugat

Catalonia Today, 3 May 2007

At a secondary school in Sant Cugat last week, one of the students secretly staged a phony riot in his classroom, filmed it, edited it, and posted it on YouTube, claiming such mêlées were an everyday occurrence at the school in question (of which he supplied the name and address).

The teachers there told me they felt insulted, humiliated even, and I could see their point. Teaching adolescents—this budding director was just fourteen—is often about as much fun as emptying a chemical toilet. For the staff, seeing their school depicted as a haven of chaos on the World Wide Web was the last straw. The culprit was expelled.

I hamfistedly played devil's advocate by insisting that what this particular teenager had done was an act of imaginative subversion worthy of Abbie Hoffman, America's best and brightest political agitator (a prime mover behind the Vietnam anti-war protests and author of a notorious guide to free living called *Steal This Book*). Expulsion, I suggested, just isn't going to work with a truly rebellious soul. The American government, for example, hounded Hoffman out of the country, but that simply spurred him to ever more spectacular acts of sedition. The school, I hinted, would do better to follow the example of the British Establishment, which, as soon as a creative rebel heaves into sight, loses no time in praising the b'jesus out of him and then rewarding him with a reputable medal, thus neutralising him completely for the rest of what would otherwise have been a richly mischievous life.

Tita in Denial

On the evil lurking behind the fortune that paid for the Thyssen-Bornemisza art collection

Catalonia Today, 10 May 2007

I have been watching the neuronically-challenged status junky that goes by the name of Carmen "Tita" Cervera for years. We all have. Ever since she crawled out of her B-movie acting career into the European aristocracy, via her 1982 marriage to the art-loving Baron Hans-Heinrich "Heini" Thyssen-Bornemisza, the Spanish media set about converting Tita into the National Institution she now is, and with a heavily capitalised 'N'. When she allowed just 75 of her and Heini's 1,300 paintings to be permanently exhibited in Barcelona, she stipulated that they would be whisked back to Madrid if Catalonia became independent (prompting some Catalans to remark that it was surely no coincidence that *tita* means *prick* in their language).

Well, the whistle on the Thyssen-Bornemisza collection has just been blown, with the recent revelation that Heini's inherited fortune was made on the backs of 10,000 slave labourers provided by the Nazis, whose favours his family fervently curried. In 1945, for example, Heini's sister Margit hosted a party for the SS at the family castle, at which her guests were invited to hunt down 200 half-starved Jewish prisoners.

Even the "donation" of Tita and Heini's partially-looted collection to Spain turns out to have been a fraud. We taxpayers chipped in 600 million dollars for what is, in effect, little more than a long-term loan.

Tita has recently been back in the the Spanish press. To apologise for her late husband's ghastly past? No, to trumpet the fact that she has saved the trees that line Madrid's Paseo del Prado from being cut down. Tears welled up in her eyes as she announced this victory, blinding her, presumably, to the ghosts of 200 murdered Jews scuttling from trunk to trunk, still trying to dodge the bullets of her sister-in-law's Nazi friends.

Matthew Tree

Seven
On a racist electoral video
in Catalonia's third biggest city
Catalonia Today, 17 May 2007

Siete minutos is an electoral propaganda video lasting as long as its title states, featuring Xavier García Albiol, the Partido Popular's mayoral candidate for Badalona. This DVD has been described by the other political parties as an incitement to racism. They do not protest enough. *Siete minutos* is possibly the most disgustingly racist film produced by a mainstream European political party since the heyday of this particular genre in 1930s Germany.

Not just because the apparently spontaneous interviewees have been carefully edited (you don't have to have worked in TV to spot this ten miles off) so that they establish a direct link between crime, immigration and—given that the current Mayoress might allow a mosque to be built on a municipal site—the usurpation by foreign elements of public land. Neither is the problem that—despite Badalona being a bilingual city (I know, I worked there for eight years)—the video is 100% in Spanish, indicating it is sneakily aimed at that reactionary minority of monolingual working-class Castilian speakers who would rather vote for ultraconservatives than for Catalan-friendly socialists.

No, what makes this a really nasty video is the repeated use of blurred, middle-distance images (accompanied by distorted Arabic music) of Moroccan people in the street, presenting them as permanently obtrusive aliens, visibly less human than the sharply focussed, close-upped white Badalonans. Jesus, even Jorg Haider would have thought twice before showing anything as chauvinistic as this.

Last week the European Parliament revealed that a handful of German, French, and British citizens resident in Catalonia had been complaining to it about the "growth of extreme Catalan nationalism". Yeah, right. Go to YouTube, you predictably misguided Aryans, and check out what Catalonia's only "anti-nationalist" party is getting up to.

The Enormity of the Tragedy

On the belated but welcome UK publication
of a novel by Catalonia's best writer

Catalonia Today, 24 May 2007

For years, I've enthused in vain to friends in London about the work of Barcelonan author Quim Monzó, one of the most original prose writers on the European continent (any Thomases doubting this seemingly extravagant claim will find it endorsed by experts far wiser than me on *http://members. tripod.com/~monzo/critica.htm*).

In vain, because my friends were unable to see for themselves if my praise was justified or not, given that Monzó—despite having sold nearly three quarters of a million books in Catalan alone, as well as having been translated into Czech, Russian, Romanian, Portuguese, Norwegian, Dutch, Japanese, Italian, Hungarian, Hebrew, Galician, French, Finnish, Spanish, Slovenian, Swedish, Danish, Basque and German—had not had a single one of his twenty-two titles published in the UK. Until now.

This June, Monzó's 1989 novel *The Enormity of the Tragedy* will be brought out by Peter Owen Publishers, London, in a fine translation by Peter Bush. For me and other English admirers of Monzó, this is news worth celebrating with larger than usual quantities of alcohol. Still, the question is begged: how could it have taken the UK publishing industry three decades to discover a major writer working in the EU's seventh largest language?

The most likely answer is that just 3% of books published in Britain are translations, effectively cutting off readers in that country from most foreign literature. Time and again, I have found that many world-class writers (such as the Nobel Prize winner Imre Kertesz, among others) are far easier to obtain in Catalan than in English.

I am often assured—by Catalans desperately eager to learn it—that my mother tongue is the international language. Out of politeness, I desist from reminding them that it's also a one-way street.

Into Africa

On the start of my first trip
out of Europe and into Africa

Catalonia Today, 1 June 2007

I am what they call a nervous traveller: the kind who takes an early dose of anti-anxiety medication then checks his passport eight times anyway, who frets and sweats in the check-out queue then tries to guyrope his fear-stricken face into a carefree expression during take-off and landing, and on arrival needs a pride of stiff drinks just to get used to his first day in a foreign country, even when he visits a nearby nation that he knows pretty much like the back of his hand, such as Holland, say. Or England.

So it isn't surprising that right now I am in a state of the sheerest pre-travel fear I have ever felt, given that I will soon be making the longest journey in my life to a place I know so little I can't even imagine it: Tanzania. And I will not be on safari.

Over the last twenty years I have written seven different versions of a novel in English, all of which are unmistakably abject failures. I am now on version eight, and am as sure as sure can be that I have finally hit upon the right track. However, in order for the novel to be credible, I need to see things from an African point of view (whatever that might turn out to be) and the only way to do that, I have realised, is to go there.

So on June 2, one nervous little middle-aged white man, his veins flowing with vaccine and probably vodka, will be winging his way into the cradle of humanity, without any real idea as to what awaits him. When I get back, I will let you know if anything was. Until then, *kwa heri, watu woto*.

Eco-Pests

On the hordes of cyclists who are making
a hell of a nuisance of themselves in Barcelona

Catalonia Today, 14 June 2007

A decade ago, there were so few of them, nobody so much as noticed. Then, in the early nineties, they increased in numbers, but were, thankfully, restricted to certain designated areas. Now, however, they are legion, they are everywhere, they take you from behind, they ram you from the front, they frown and grumble when they find their right of way blocked by toddlers who they have been on the point of turning into flattened flesh, they wing pedestrians without a word of apology and defy red lights and one-way signs as if to the manner born. I am talking, of course, about the growing hordes of Barcelona cyclists thanks to whom you now stroll at your peril.

It all started as a bit of harmless pro-environment symbolism invented by the Olympic Mayor, Pasqual Maragall, who introduced *El Dia de la Bici*, on which everybody could go pedal-crazy for just one day a year. This proved so popular that Maragall, taking his cue from Amsterdam, then ordered whole kilometres of white lines to be daubed across our pavements in a poor man's version of the purpose-built *fietspaden* that criss-cross the Dutch capital. Well, it's a fine mess he's got us into.

Perhaps the only solution left is to lobby for a Bicycle-Free Day, on which it would, briefly, be politically cool to tell people obsessed with carbon footprints to get off their bikes. How wonderful it would then be for us pedestrians to have twenty-four hours during which we wouldn't have to cross bicycle paths with thumping hearts, eyes peeled for any sign of a ruthless eco-warrior going like the clappers.

Matthew Tree

The Unhappy Rock

On prisoners ashamed about how normal people
will see them once they're released

Catalonia Today, 14 June 2007

The last time I had the luck to be invited to a prison—on this occasion, *Quatre Camins*, a.k.a *La Roca*, the internees' preferred name for the place— the same thing happened as has happened on all such visits: once the official talk (my talk) had been given, the real talk began. As ever, it was more varied and fascinating than anything I'd managed to come up with. The audience chatted, for example, about atheism and the late-night bars on Barcelona's Carrer Escudellers, and painting pictures in jail and, last but not least, the harshness of prison life, and the media's systematic covering up of the same.

This particular visit, a fortnight ago, was atypical, in that I was with the "privileged" end of La Roca's population: internees who are in a half-way wing from which they are allowed out on controlled occasions to get them used to their final release, within a year or so.

Mainly young people, all were arrested for drugs-related misdemeanours. None of them had caused anyone any grievous psychological or bodily harm, and yet the authorities could think of nothing better than to lock them up tight for several years with men who had. They feel frustrated at having been given such an unjustifiably tough deal, but far worse is the indelible stain they fear a prison record represents for the majority of normal people lurking disapprovingly in the outside world. I still regret not having been able to tell them something that only occurred to me later in the day: that having survived what they've survived makes them different, special even, and that they have a right to be proud of precisely that. Just who the hell do "normal people" think they are, anyway?

The Tanzanian TV Interview
On learning to learn from Tanzanian television
Catalonia Today, 21 June 2007

Anyone might reasonably think that a person coming back from his first visit to Africa—as I did a week ago today—would feel an overriding need to gush the gush that Africa inspires in so many of us Europeans. About the dignity of poverty-stricken Africans who have to improvise their livelihoods, for example, or about their natural tendency to laugh (unmarred by Western Sophistication), or the sad cuteness of weary African school kids. That kind of gush.

But the first impression that truly got my attention on my recent Tanzanian trip, was an interview on Tanzanian television. I was watching a Swahili sitcom, convinced by previously chugged Tusker beer that I could catch its gist, when suddenly a chat show host popped up speaking in English. This he did because his guest that day was the South African diplomat Thandi Lujabe-Rankoe. At first I merely gawped at the curious spectacle of two people talking with fluent irony in a third language about years of pale-faced oppression familiar to both, but eventually noticed that this interview was taking a blissfully long time, time not being an issue for an underfunded TV station. As a result, I felt I was coming to know Ms Lujabe-Rankoe's extraordinary life—she had fought against apartheid since her teenage years—exceptionally well, and was getting more out of this one in-depth conversation than I had from years and years of sound-bite geared chats on English, Catalan, and Spanish talk shows. How wonderful, if someone here decided to learn from this Tanzanian way of interviewing. How wonderful, it suddenly struck me, if we really realised, in this case and others, that the most surprising things can be learnt from countries we have forever been used to treating as slow pupils.

Matthew Tree

Africans Wear Watches, Too

On how a trip to Tanzania put paid to several pernicious European clichés about the African continent

29 June 2007

About a fortnight ago me and a Tanzanian nurse called Margareth Mwakeye were waiting for the manager of the Vyana Dance Troupe in Mkurunga, a village near Dar-es-Salaam. He was late. People often are, Margareth said, what with the poor roads and the dala-dala bus system: privately-run Toyota Hi Aces whose drivers, in order to break even, refuse to set off until their passengers are packed tighter than battery hens before setting off. Margareth added, with a smile, that whenever she arrived late for work at her NGO, her European colleagues would tell her not to worry, assuring her that Africans "had a different sense of time". She was still chuckling at this groundless cliché—which I had taken for granted until a second ago—when the manager turned up, tutting at his watch and apologising profusely for the delay.

He took us to see his troupe: nineteen young people who combine traditional ritual dances with contemporary lyrics about the dangers of AIDS, because, here as in all poor countries, hordes of non-professional, poorly-informed local girls sleep with men for money—infected truck-drivers mostly—including housewives who, in their desperate attempts to provide food at home, inadvertently end up passing on the virus to their husbands and future children.

As soon as I started watching the troupe at work, another of my preconceptions about the continent went up in smoke: traditional African dancing, when seen up close, was not, as I had previously supposed, a lot of stomping made attractive by the performers' ingenuous energy, but a highly complicated series of choreographical relays, executed with a disarming ease that belied years of rehearsal.

Over the next few days, yet another, more general, African myth of mine was blown out of the water. Ever since the first images of the Biafran war appeared on a TV set that my parents hastened to switch off (concerned at the effect of a live genocide on a nine year-old mind), I had been conditioned by European news bulletins to see Africa as little more than a breeding-ground for insoluble catastrophes. So it had come as a shock to discover that large swathes of the African continent—Tanzania included—live in a perfectly ordinary state of peace.

Best of all, on the final day, my very last cliché about Africa, as stubborn as it was irrational, was also proven resoundingly false. I had had the luck to meet Erick Shigongo, Tanzania's best-known writer, who has created his huge readership from scratch by serialising his novels à la Dickens in various Swahili tabloids, then publishing them, when completed, in book form. Bookshops being few and far between, he sells his books through street vendors, with publicity being provided by the tabloids' district reps around the country. So it is, that in a country where just over 30% of the population is still illiterate, Shigongo manages to sell an average of 75,000 copies per title.

He now has his eyes on the international market, but has discovered a major obstacle: in Europe a lot of people seriously don't think that Africans are capable of writing books; in fact, he added, a lot of people out there don't think Africans can think at all. By now he was laughing out loud, and I was, too, louder than him, even, because, hard as I find to admit it, I had on occasion entertained thoughts such as the ones he was laughing so loudly about—breathed them in for nearly fifty years together with the vapid European air, in fact—and now, at last, I had been released from such absurd and potentially evil notions, released for good in Erick Shigongo's pleasant patio as we threw our heads back and roared with laughter at all those dumb white fools who were unable to credit Africans with the ability to write fiction, unable to credit Africans even with a single original thought.

Thanks be to Tanzania, I had just found out in person that such fools can be cured for good.

Tour de Dunce

On the inexplicable habit tourists have
of dressing oddly when abroad

Catalonia Today, 29 June 2007

As is notoriously known, all over the world people who dress and behave normally at home—blending like chameleons into their native milieus—feel the need to make themselves more conspicuous than an entire busload of court jesters as soon as they visit a foreign country for pleasure.

Anyone who remembers the late seventies, when Barcelona was barely a dot on anybody's map, will find it hard to forget those tourists who were occasionally bussed in from the Costa Brava and used to wander along the Passeig de Gràcia in swimming trunks and bikinis, oblivious to the fact that everyone else was in full office wear. Even now, many of the plentiful weekend trippers to the city still wear clothes that make them look—to quote a local simile—as odd as octopae in a garage.

But I never realised the extremes some tourists are capable of until I went to Dar-es-Salaam a fortnight ago. The local dress code is crystal clear: smart T-shirts, long trousers, and absolutely no hats. On my first day, in one of the side streets off Kariakoo Market, I found myself gawping in astonishment at two tourists who were twinned up in identical open-necked shirts, Baden Powell style baggy shorts, and baseball caps with peaks as obtrusive as toucan beaks. They looked so bizarre it was a moment before I realised that on top of everything else they were as white as I was. In a nutshell, they couldn't have stood out more in that African neighbourhood if they'd gone as Laa-Laa and Tinky Winky. No wonder they were being eyed closely by all the locals, whose perfectly natural curiosity was, for some reason, visibly scaring them out of their globe-trotting wits.

Frankly, My Dear

On the need for putting the Frankfurt controversy
behind us and promoting the books instead

Catalonia Today, 5 July 2007

Wednesday, June 27th saw the official presentation in Barcelona of the *Projecte Frankfurt*, which involves sending well over a hundred Catalan-language authors from seven different countries (and four different Spanish autonomous communities) to the Frankfurt Book Fair—the largest of its kind in the world—in October, with a view to putting Catalan literature (the Fair's "Special Guest" this year) on the international map.

As my paper neighbour Frederic Barberà pointed out in his good article last week, whenever Spain is the guest at events of this kind, there is not so much as a mote of dissonance in the air: only Spanish language writers get to go, and that's that (as happened a few months ago at the London Book Fair). But woe betide the Catalans should they attempt to make a similar move: despite the internationally vouched-for scientific definition of Catalan literature as literature written in Catalan, and even though several Catalan writers working in Spanish had been invited but had voluntarily declined to go, howls of outrage went up in Madrid when it was finally announced that only Catalan-language authors would be flying to Frankfurt. So much had these howls upset the Projecte Frankfurt organisers speaking at the presentation last Wednesday, that instead of putting all this negative noise behind them they preferred to jerk their knees in an excruciatingly dull political response, heavily larded with words such as "nation", "persecution", and "cultural genocide", which were not at all called for at that time and place. And there were us writers in the audience, thinking they were going to talk about books, for heaven's sake. Here's hoping they start doing so by the time we get to Frankfurt, because I, for once, do not want to be there just for the beer.

Matthew Tree

Wedding Hell
On the superfluity of marriage

Catalonia Today, 12 July 2007

The other day I watched my Mum's birthday present, a 1950 Spencer Tracy classic called *Father of the Bride*, the story of a middle-class father who finds that the budget for his daughter's wedding is spiralling out of control as more and more trimmings are added to what was originally supposed to be a simple ceremony. It turned out to be one of those wisp-light American comedies, with a humour so gentle you barely notice it brushing past you, but which can still tickle full-throated laughter out of viewers, sixty years on.

Not least, because, sixty years on, many people are still behaving like Spencer Tracy's ridiculous daughter. Although marriage is now effectively little more than an optional caprice in a Europe that doesn't blink once at common-law couples, people of all ages have not yet managed to ditch the habit of spending wheelbarrows full of money to put a seal of spurious public legitimacy on relationships which by definition are purely private matters.

Like most people over forty, I have been subjected to more than my fair share of these senseless ceremonies, watching, bemused, as godless couples that have been fornicating together for years, step out of the church door beaming in anticipation of the First Night. What is this mental virus that lies dormant for years before jumping up and obliging people to go through their parents' motions? At this rate, the same couples—when their marriages run onto the inevitable rocks—will start refusing to get divorced "for the sake of the children", a traditional excuse at least as old as marriage itself. I, for one, hope things don't get to that stage. For the sake of the children.

Love is the Dope
On the need to give God a holiday
Catalonia Today, 21 July 2007

Last week, 140 inhabitants of the town of Emerli, Iraq, who belong to a religious sect, were bombed to death by neighbours belonging to another religious sect. In Islamabad, Pakistan, following an assault on a mosque occupied by armed religious people who wished to impose religious law on the entire country, more religious people have just blown up two dozen Pakistani conscripts in protest. In Qalai Sadan, Afghanistan, holy-minded militiamen who for religious reasons believe women should not be educated, machine-gunned a schoolgirl for having gone to school.

According to the *Journal of Neurophysiology* (May, 2005) exorbitant feelings of love can affect the dopamine level in the brain to a degree that can lead to highly irrational, even psychotic behaviour. Exorbitant love of God is no exception, if last week's evidence alone is anything to go by.

The atrocities mentioned above happen to have been carried out in the name of Islam, but I for one do not doubt that the denomination is immaterial. Any faith, if taken in excessive quantities, can turn your average pious chump into a hatchet man. From 1991 to 1995, for example, one of the nastiest civil wars in Europe featured entire armies of true-believers whose spree killings and rapings were blessed by local Catholic and Orthodox authorities.

Indeed, wherever religion flourishes, there shall we find whole skiploads of dogma-based suffering, all of it imposed on behalf of supernatural entities whose existence is asserted without evidence and who may, therefore—as Christopher Hitchens puts it—be dismissed without evidence, too. In which case, why don't we all give God the summer off, just for the hell of it? I'm sure He'd appreciate the break.

Catalland

On Dutch people's current (unwitting) penchant for Catalan writers

Catalonia Today, 6 September 2007

I couldn't get away from them. Whether in the canal-ridden village of Monnickendam or in the heart of Amsterdam, whether in the market town of Hoorn or the tourist trap of Marken, I kept running into earshot of Catalan speakers throughout my holiday in Holland. They seemed to have infiltrated the Dutch summer, slapdash spies who gave themselves away time and again with loud greetings of *bon dia* followed by a conspiratorial grin.

Far more unusual, though, was the sight—unprecedented in the fifteen years I've been visiting the Netherlands—of Catalan language authors on display in every single bookshop window I peeked at, and I peeked at plenty. They all showed *Het Geluk [La felicitat/Happiness]*, a fat novel about pre-war Barcelona by Lluís-Anton Baulenas and some had *De onzichtbare stad [La ciutat invisible/The Invisible City]*, Emili Rosales's historical mystery set in the Ebre delta. Also present was a new translation of *Colometa*, the name by which the Dutch know Mercè Rodoreda's 1962 classic *La plaça del Diamant* (which in English was published as *The Time of the Doves*).

Despite all this, I found that most Dutch people I met were still blissfully oblivious to the existence of Catalan itself, let alone its literary culture. An ignorance which the above-mentioned books only served to maintain, given that their blurbs omitted to mention the tongue they were written in, while disingenuously assuring readers that they formed part of *Spaanse literatuur*.

I sometimes wonder what would have happened if, back in the 17th century, the Netherlanders had lost, and the Catalans won, their respective wars against the Castilian occupiers. Probably Dutch, not Catalan, would now be the hidden language of Europe. And Amsterdam's *Damplein*, and not Barcelona's *Rambla*, would now be thronged with tourists using Spanish phrase books to buy Mexican hats.

Saying Goodbye to God
A look at four recent best-selling anti-God books
Catalonia Today, 6 September 2007

A review of: *Breaking the Spell—Religion as a Natural Phenomenon*, by Daniel C. Dennett. Penguin Books, 2007; *The God Delusion*, by Richard Dawkins. Bantam Press, 2006; *The End of Faith—Religion, Terror, and the Future of Reason*, by Sam Harris. Free Press, 2006; *God is not Great—The Case Against Religion*, by Christopher Hitchens. Atlantic Books, 2007.

Until recently, we unbelievers never felt any need to defend or proclaim our utter lack of faith. For us, religion—all of it—is a cupboard both locked and bare, and is no more an option for us than astrology would be for an astronomer, or witchcraft for a surgeon. In the last three years, however, four authors—the geneticist Richard Dawkins, the philosophers Sam Harris and Daniel Dennett, and the journalist Christopher Hitchens—have decided both to denounce the patent absurdity (according to them) of organised religion and to declare the non-existence of god to be a fact of life that is at once desirable and undeniable.

These writers leave no doubt that they have been driven to this by what they see as the increasing intrusion of religion into both the public and private spheres, thus holding the most basic freedoms hostage to various unprovable, primitive and often fatuous dogmas. Hardly surprising, then, that beneath the wealth of facts and arguments they offer with the relentless coolness of a professional butler, there runs an undercurrent of fury at the chutzpah of the faithful, which occasionally bursts to the surface in the form of a snide aside (as in Hitchens's go at "creationist yokels") or bitter sarcasm, or Harris's raspberry at the Muslim afterlife: "...the most sexually repressive people found in the world today...are lured to martyrdom by a conception of paradise that resembles nothing so much as an *al-fresco bordello*".

Another common element to be found in these books is their diagnosis of the flaws of organised religion: its privileged status, whereby criticisms or jibes that would be considered par for the course if applied to political or personal beliefs, become unacceptably "offensive" when levelled at faith-based ones; the countless contradictions, textual incongruities and evidence

Matthew Tree

of arbitrary compilation in all the holy books, which make nonsense of the divine authority their respective priesthoods claim for them; the redundancy of religion as a key to the understanding of the world, given that in the time that has passed since the founding of the world's major creeds, science has accurately accounted for everything the scriptures purport to explain in divine terms; and the fact that ethical behaviour, far from being predicated on religion, is an innate human quality that religion has often perverted for its own ends, spurring otherwise decent people to acts of senseless evil.

Similar though these books are on both tone and content, each covers some territory that the others overlook. Dennett, for instance, stresses that, for him, religious belief is a negative spin-off of the positive, genetically-programmed childhood need to both love and obey (it is no coincidence that most believers have their faith inculcated at an early age). Dawkins offers a potted history of the damage religion has caused and is still causing to scientific progress. Harris comes up with a surprisingly heartfelt defence of meditation as an answer to spiritual needs. Hitchens is alone in commenting on the many atrocities committed by Catholic priests in Rwanda and supposedly nirvana-savvy Buddhists in Sri Lanka.

These are serious texts, written by people who knew that after publication they would receive the countless death threats they are currently being subjected to. The only objection an atheist reader could make to these books are their very uneven styles. About one third of Dennett's *Breaking The Spell* consists of long-winded speculative questions. Dawkins switches irritatingly back and forth between US and UK English in his *The God Delusion*. In *The End of Faith*, Harris piles on anecdote after anecdote with bewildering eagerness. Hitchens punctuates his *God Is Not Great* with a modesty that is wince-makingly false ("...even a pygmy such as myself can claim to know more...").

The conclusion reached by all of them is that faith is gradually weakening its grip on the human race. As Hitchens puts it: "...the devotions of today are only the echoing repetitions of yesterday, sometimes ratcheted up to screaming point so as to ward off the terrible emptiness". Religion, in other words, is slowly but surely on its way out, and the current rise of warmongering theocrats in both East and West is the start of its long goodbye. It is up to us, so Dawkins and the others imply, to make sure that it ends not with a bang but a whimper.

S.O.S.

On stool samples

Catalonia Today, 14 September 2007

Not long ago, I went to my local *Centre d'Atenció Primària* (health clinic) with a badly upset stomach. The doctor told me the first thing she needed was an analysis of several *mostres de femta*—literally, *showings of dung*, the Catalan medical term for what English so politely calls *stools*—and handed me three plastic containers.

Already, I'm probably sharing far more with you than you wish to know, so I won't go into the details of how I managed to get the samples into the pots. Suffice to say that I found back issues of my usual newspaper, the *Avui*, indispensable. When the appointed day of collection came, I went back to the C.A.P., plumped a dark plastic bag holding my samples in front of one of the administrative nurses and discreetly hissed: *Tres mostres de femta.* "What?" she snapped. I raised my voice to a stage whisper: *Tres mostres de femta!* A nearby group of patients turned to look. The nurse tutted. My dung, she loudly informed me (and them) had missed the collection time and was no longer usable. Blushing cherry-red, I mumbled a request for replacement pots, which she duly plonked down on the counter. I gathered them up, together with my little cargo of redundant crap, and left the building, watched with commiseration by what was now a small audience.

It wasn't until I got home that the humiliation of having my own faeces rejected in public hit me like a chunk of aircraft waste. Bodily functions are like that: they can so often make mincemeat of your ego. Which is surely why mine decided to run away altogether for one very long and wobbly day. As the American saying so rightly—and tritely—says: shit happens.

Matthew Tree

Mirror, Mirror

On why Scotland has a potentially rosier future than Catalonia

Catalonia Today, 23 September 2007

A remarkable wee essay appeared in the bookshops recently: *El mirall escocès [The Scottish Mirror]*, an insider's comparison of the current political situation in both Scotland and Catalonia, written by Xavier Solano, a Barcelona-born political adviser to the Scottish National Party.

Nestling in chapter four is a fascinating explanation of the key difference between Britain and Spain as far as the "national question" is concerned. According to Solano, although England incorporated the Welsh into the UK by main force, and the Scots by bamboozling them into signing a contract, it never tried to make either nation officially English. By contrast, Castile, after its 18th century subjugation of the peninsular periphery, claimed the umbrella denomination "Spain" as a synonym for itself, and then set about hammering those territories that gave the lie to this blatant bit of bluffing, into the Castilian national mould. This accounts for why Thatcher, Major, and Blair can publicly accept a hypothetical independent Scotland, whereas Aznar, Rajoy, and Zapatero would sooner drown themselves in a tub full of pigs' diarrhoea than even hint at the possibility of a sovereign Catalonia or Euskadi. Their Spain—being based on a lexical falsehood—is an object of faith, a sacred unity, the obvious heterogeneity of whose disparate parts is to be disregarded at all costs. Hence the Castilian monopoly on the word *nation*, the supersized Spanish flags that have to be flown everywhere, the ludicrous deference afforded the monarchy and the sabre-rattling whenever Basques or Catalans come up with a wheeze for achieving more autonomy. As a result, Scotland may well become self-governing in the near future; whereas Catalonia, follow though it might in the same democratic footsteps as its northern equivalent, will almost certainly find itself looking into the barrel of a gun.

If It Works, Don't Touch It

On the endless offers to enlarge penises

Catalonia Today, 27 September 2007

In the whole wide world, there is now not a single man, woman or child with an internet connection, who has not been asked if he or she would like his or her penis enlarged. Most people—excepting those sad gentlemen who really believe that a modified todger will bring a permanent ray of sunshine into their lives—automatically consign these johnson-obsessed inducements to the trash.

Recently, however, these messages have been getting increasingly close to the bone. The other day I was informed personally ("Morning matthewtree") by one Panzaru Marchetti that his "cock" was "soooo big now, thanks to these doctors". This is far more information than I require, given that I have never been the slightest bit curious about the phallic status of even my closest male friends, let alone that of a pseudonymous stranger.

The next schlong-oriented message turned out to be a good deal more personal, at least at first sight. A certain Moose Foluke was itching to find out: "Did you ever ask yourself is my penis big enough?" At first, I thought it bizarre that Mr Foluke assumed I would be concerned about the size of his manhood, until it dawned on me that, like so many people with large ones, he had lost the ability to punctuate. Put a colon or a comma in the middle of the sentence, though, and it becomes clear that it is my own wang he is referring to. The answer to this question, Moose, is most definitely no. Those of us belonging to the pre-pornography generation know that it's not what you have, it's what you do that counts. OK, MF? My apologies, by the by, to readers who find this a distasteful subject. I just fancied playing about a bit with my own column, this being its sixty-ninth appearance in *Catalonia Today*.

Rude Boys
On the importance of telling the Bourbons
to bugger off
Catalonia Today, 4 October 2007

Back in 1970, the American writer William Burroughs wrote that Britain would not be a free country until all its citizens rose as one and screamed out "BUGGER THE QUEEN!" Seven years later he had the satisfaction of telegramming his personal congratulations to the Sex Pistols for having done something very similar with their single "God Save The Queen", probably the most passionate symbolic attack on a constitutional monarchy, ever: "God save the queen/the fascist regime.../God save the queen/she "ain't no human being". It went straight to number two in the charts.

Meanwhile, here in Spainland, three decades later, two young Catalan left-wingers who set light to a photograph of the local monarch and his lady wife during a recent demonstration in Girona, were hauled up before a court in the state capital and are now likely to get between six months and two years of porridge for "insulting the King". These formal accusations sparked off further protests around Catalonia—at which yet more royal mugshots were enthusiastically consigned to the flames—spurring the pertinent judges in Madrid to demand identification of all the people involved (about 300) so that they, too, could be duly accused of rudeness to his Highness. As a result, further protests have been planned, and so it goes on.

Meanwhile, the rest of the planet is about to celebrate the 30th anniversary of the release of the Sex Pistols' "God Save The Queen", on October 8th. By way of a contribution to this homage, I would like to follow in William Burroughs's footsteps and recommend that on the day in question, Catalans everywhere practice a little English rudeness of their own by rising to their feet as one nation and bellowing: "BUGGER THE BOURBONS!" I wonder if anyone'll notice?

Then We Took Berlin

On how it would be so very nice if official Spain
confessed to Franco's crimes

Catalonia Today, 11 October 2007

Berlin is dotted with Holocaustian landmarks, such as the flower-strewn plaque that marks the spot where Tiergartenstrasse 4 used to be: the building out of which the Nazis organised the gassing and starvation of 110,000 mentally handicapped Germans; or the sumptuous house by Wannsee lake where a conference chaired by Reinhard Heydrich in early 1942 put the final seal of approval on a pre-existing order to liquidate 11 million European Jews. I visited both memorial sites last week, came to the verge of tears, and then went about my business.

My business being a round table at the local Instituto Cervantes, together with the Czech Monika Zgustova, the Argentinian Patrícia Gabancho and the Moroccan Najat El Hachmi, Catalan language authors all. We talked to an enthusiastic audience about how come we had chosen to work in a non-mother tongue. Afterwards, we celebrated over a drink or two. Given that the Salamanca Archive controversy—the refusal of the Spanish government to return documents looted 70 years ago by Franco's troops, to their rightful owners—had been much in the news before we left for Berlin, we couldn't help but compare the filibustering in Madrid with the highly visible amends the Germans have made for their own fascist past, thus giving them the historical self-awareness required for a definitive shift to a democratic system. By contrast, Spain's reluctance to officially atone for Franco's crimes has allowed the very hobbyhorse on which that little man rode into power, to dominate the political agenda once again: national unity at all costs. This is both saddening and maddening, given that the costs were paid long ago— including those stolen papers in Salamanca, used to incriminate and execute—and the victims haven't yet been given so much as a receipt.

Matthew Tree

Grand Hotel
On getting into my Frankfurt hotel
Catalonia Today, 18 October 2007

We got into Frankfurt on the night of October 9th, a half-hour too late to catch Quim Monzó's razor-stroke of an opening speech at the Book Fair. There were three of us: a Catalan-speaking oral literature expert from Benin, a translator into Catalan from Slovenia and the fat-faced bastard whose photo (in the print version) is at the top of this article. We were let out in front of a dry-docked ocean liner of a hotel behind the desk of which three receptionists awaited us, placed neatly at metre intervals, their welcome grins already in place.

We were grilled simultaneously about our addresses, birthdays, and whatnot before being handed a key card which, they warned to our surprise, we also needed for the lift.

In which we spent a good twenty minutes, because I simply could not master the knack of inserting the card and marking our floor in the right sequence ("You're behaving like an African!" joked Agnès, the Beninese). Anyhow, I finally made it to a luxurious walk-in freezer of a room, slept badly, woke early, and wandered over to the window. Before me, a Trade Fair building lurked in the dawn like a gigantic metal-scaled louse. Behind it, a row of its taller sister buildings stuck fuck-you fingers up at the mongrel-coloured sky. So, I had finally laid eyes on the Frankfurt Book Fair: the hub of the publishing world, the Mecca of international literature. Like my companions, I had a unique opportunity to do some potentially vital networking in this inhospitable, plug-ugly sprawl.

Clutching my key card, I made for the door and consoled myself with the thought that whatever I was about to do, I would not have the chance to do it again for a long, long time.

How Does It Feel?

On the similarity between anarchist band CRASS and the Valencian singer Raimon

Catalonia Today, 25 October 2007

Those Barcelona residents with a little cash in their pockets could do worse than blow it on a low-cost ticket to London for the weekend starting November 24th, when some ex-members of the anarchist band CRASS—the only musicians in rock history who really believed their own lyrics—will be performing at the Shepherd's Bush Empire.

I saw them play just once, in an abandoned warehouse in south London, in 1982. They never advertised their shows (or anything else), but word of mouth had packed the place to the gills with all kinds of spectators, including a sprinkling of plainclothes police officers (belied by their newsreader haircuts and hissing coat lapels).

Vocalist Steve Ignorant began by screaming about starving children drowning in businessmen's bowls of corn flakes as twin back-projecting screens merged images of cosmetics ads with bloated-bellied kids from Africa. An hour or so after this entrée, while the banned anti-Falklands war single addressed to Mrs Thatcher—*How does it feel to be the mother of a thousand dead?/Young boys rest now, cold graves in cold earth*—was being roared, even the constables looked impressed by CRASS's mix of intelligent protest and sheer rage. I thought I would never hear anything like it again. Until just last Sunday, when, in the Palau Sant Jordi, before 12,000 citizens outraged by the refusal of the central government to make amends for its fascist past, the curiously punkish-looking singer-songwriter Raimon (Xàtiva, 1940) belted out hair-electrifying versions of some of his best protest songs, sending this listener back 25 years to the London warehouse where he had once stood thrilled, thrilled to bits by his first taste ever of music made solely to get the truth—or at least a truth—across.

Bad-Being

On the natural paranoia that comes from publishing a book about religion

Catalonia Today, 6 November 2007

About a year and a half ago I wrote a piece for this column about the paranoia that besets many writers when they bring out a new book. During the first crucial month, eager to know how the book in question is faring, they find themselves hanging so desperately on any word—good, bad or ugly—concerning it, that their nerves end up as frayed as a cat's blanket. There is probably no apter noun for what they feel than the Catalan (and Spanish) *malestar*.

In the case of my own most recently published book, *La vida després de Déu [Life After God]*, there is yet another factor to be taken into account. Given that it is opposed to all organised religions, it is almost bound to offend at least a few people, some of whom will, inevitably, be of an aggressive bent. A situation which has me trapped between the usual desire to see the book do well—which would increase the possibility that the wrong people get to hear about it—and a fervent, dread-driven wish that everybody forgets about it as soon as possible.

Recently it struck me that I could have the worst of both worlds. Sod's law—the only supernatural entity experience has taught me to respect—might well ensure that the book sells hardly any copies, but that one of these will, by some ghastly chance, fall into the hands of one of those believers so true that he (or she) feels impelled to dispense with my presence on a permanent basis. I have already taken a few simple precautions, to be on the safe side. After all, as the London anarchists used to say, just because you're paranoid doesn't mean they're not watching you.

All the Time

On a good friend's reaction to
a bit of anti-Catalan bullshit

Catalonia Today, 8 November 2007

Last Sunday, me and Max, my best friend in London and the entire UK, for that matter, arranged to meet up at the Apple Store in Regent Street. When I got there, he ess-em-essed me to say he'd be a little late. Already a touch homesick after a couple of days in London, I decided to look at a Barcelona newspaper on one of the demonstration MacBooks.

Max showed up as I was browsing the sports section: "Anything of interest?" I translated a headline: "Schuster blames Madrid's defeat by Seville on the fact the referee was Catalan." Max grimaced on the spot: "Jesus, that's disgusting." "Oh," I said, revelling in the blitheness 23 years of life in Catalonia has rubbed off on me, "we get this shit all the time."

Max had come across a little of it himself. His several Spanish friends in London were all great people, he said, but he only had to tell them he had a friend who lived in Catalonia, for them to instantly express facial disapproval and on occasion even urge Max to describe my home simply as Barcelona, thus avoiding the (for them) dreaded C-word.

Such prejudice aroused Max's interest to the extent that nowadays, whenever introduced to someone from Spain, he instantly mentions his English friend in Catalonia (taking care to stress the word). If the Spaniard in question winces or flinches, Max experimentally rubs it in by explaining that this friend of his also speaks Catalan. Should this elicit further negative reactions, Max goes the whole hog, adding that his friend (me) doesn't feel he's living in Spain, wants Catalan independence, writes in Catalan etc. etc. Having thus lit the touch paper, Max stands calmly back and watches the fireworks, at once baffled and intrigued.

Matthew Tree

Out of Spirits

On television's hidden need for booze

Catalonia Today, 19 November 2007

Last week, I met up with some friends to talk about their project for a laid-back, open-ended TV chat show for a local channel. I suggested that to create an informal atmosphere, there should be some kind of alcoholic beverage available on the set. Beer, for instance. They guffawed: "Maybe back in the 1970s," they said, "but they'd never let us do that now."

Which reminded me of a woman I'd known who used to work for the BBC—back in the 1970s, precisely—whose job consisted solely of plying guests on talk shows with liquor until they were sufficiently well-oiled to be able to chat to the presenter with easy familiarity, their stage fright doused out of existence.

Indeed, back then, booze seemed to be a vital ingredient of TV life in general. One Sunday this woman friend invited me along to a party thrown by some of her colleagues. The only drinks on offer were chocolate daiquiris laden with so much rum they could have exploded on impact. After a few of these, one man went tipsily bananas, hollering obscenity after obscenity at anyone who crossed his path. The next day, I saw him on the small screen. He was reading the sports news with a smile as measured as his words. It struck me that television is an exceptionally hypocritical medium, forever keeping hermetically mum about what goes on behind its squeaky-clean scenes. If this Catalan chat show I mentioned gets off the ground, the powers that be will no doubt ditch the visible beer idea—on the grounds it would be a politically incorrect incitement to alcohol consumption—thus obliging their guests to hastily chug down as many bottles as they require, just before the cameras roll.

It's That Man Again

On teaching the King of Spain some manners

Catalonia Today, 22 November 2007

Earlier this month the Minister of Education, Mercedes Cabrera, decided that *civismo* (civic manners) needed to be taught as a compulsory subject in all secondary schools, in an attempt to stem what local observers perceive to be a rising Spain-wide tide of unacceptably uncouth adolescent behaviour.

The Minister added the caveat that there were doubts among those in charge of preparing the course material as to how to go about instilling an abstract code of values in half a million highly material teenagers.

Indeed, in Spain's recent educational history, civic manners have been taught at school-level to just one person alone: John Charles Alfonse Victor Mary of Bourbon and Bourbon-Two Sicilies—better known in Catalonia as Joan Carles I—was brought up to be nothing if not polite. Born in Rome, the future King of Spain was groomed in the finest etiquette from an early age at exclusive private schools in Switzerland and Portugal. When he finally arrived in Spain, at the age of ten, he continued his studies in another expensive school, this time in Madrid, from which he graduated to elite military academies in Saragossa, Pontevedra, and San Javier in Murcia where he presumably learnt the importance of discipline and restraint. The result? Before the entire world, at the Ibero-American Summit in Santiago, Chile, on November 11th, this sacred head of an increasingly dysfunctional family, who (officially) represents over 40 million Spanish citizens, turned to a politician (officially) representing 26 million Venezuelans, and snarled the Spanish equivalent of "shaddapaya face". If I were Mercedes Cabrera, I'd drop the idea of teaching civic manners. If it hasn't worked for the King himself, it's hardly going to work for all his foul-talking, street-burping, binge-drinking teenage subjects, now is it?

Matthew Tree

Not in Front of the Foreigners
On La Caixa's peculiar telephonic treatment
of foreign people
Catalonia Today, 1 December 2007

The other day my girlfriend called up the home insurance department of the Caixa d'Estalvis i Pensions de Barcelona, to see if they would cough up for a burst pipe in the kitchen. A recorded voice offered her a choice of languages: Catalan, Castilian, French, German, or English. She pressed Catalan. The voice then requested her DNI number. She gave it and was again asked for her language of preference, but this time, to her surprise, Catalan had been dropped from the list. She pushed Castilian and finally got a sentient human being on the other end of the line. On inquiring why the Catalan option was no longer available, she was informed that her ID number revealed she was a foreigner (she is, indeed, Dutch) and so naturally wouldn't know Catalan.

She was flabbergasted, not least by the fact that this ridiculous linguistic policy was being implemented by Catalonia's flagship bank. Ridiculous, because if in our own small circle of friends alone, there are Catalan-speakers from Ireland, Germany, Peru, Tanzania, Morocco, France, Italy, Argentina, and the United States of America, then in the Principality at large there are doubtless scores of thousands more. What is worse, it's not just the Caixa which finds the existence of such people inconceivable: many Catalans have a dazzlingly obtuse tendency to instantly switch to Spanish as soon as they clock that the other person wasn't born within the sight of Montserrat. We *gastarbeiters* could be forgiven for occasionally feeling that it's us and us alone—or some of us, at least—who are keeping the language alive and kicking, even as the locals blame us for hounding it into an early grave.

Socks

On writing (and talking) badly about sex

Catalonia Today, 9 December 2007

Whenever one of their married friends went in for a bit of adultery, many folk of my parents' generation would come out with a phrase both knowing and damning: "sex has raised its ugly head". Teetering on the precipice of adolescence as I then was, hypothetical copulation was much on my mind, but the grown-ups would only have to say that unpleasant line about sex's head, and my budding erotic thoughts would flee for a fortnight at least: an unfortunate choice of words, I realised, can stun the libido at source.

As has been proven annually in the UK since 1993 by the Bad Sex in Fiction Awards (organised by *The Literary Review*). This year's shortlist included some off-putting descriptions of the vagina: "a powerful ethnic muscle scented by bitter lemon" according to novelist Gary Steyngart, or: "...this ancient avenue...pulling at my prick like a lodestone" in the words of fellow writer Christopher Rush. But enough of muff: here is full sex as seen by Ali Smith in her new novel *Boy Meets Girl*: "we hit heart, we hit home, we were the tail of a fish, the reek of a cat...". The late Norman Mailer eventually won the 2007 prize, with a description of Adolf Hitler's brother's penis: "as soft as a coil of excrement".

A group of Catalan admirers of the Bad Sex Awards are currently looking for local candidates. Personally, I don't think they'll find anything to beat the following poem by singer Celdoni Fonoll: *Jo m'escorro, tu t'escorres/quina escorreguda, déus!/m'has buidat la iogurtera/i m'has deixat KO, Neus*. Need an emergency ghastly image to delay orgasm at the crucial moment? Translate this, and—as the old saying used to go—Bob's your uncle, Fanny's your aunt.

Matthew Tree

Crusty Scab

On how a socialist faction wishes to purge the Catalan public media

Catalonia Today, 13 December 2007

On December 1st, some half million people took part in the third largest demonstration Barcelona has seen since the death of Franco. Unlike its two single-issue predecessors—the pro-Autonomy demo of 1977 and the anti-Iraq-war one of 2003—this year's protest was fuelled by a myriad of different local grievances: surreptitious overtaxation, decades of public underinvestment, inexplicable power cuts, an inefficient, non-intercontinental airport, and the worst commuter train service on the European continent, among others.

It's true there were several independentist groups present, but the vast majority of marchers were as heterogeneous as the wrongs they were denouncing, united only by their awareness that the shabby and occasionally deceitful treatment they had been getting from Madrid had something to do with the fact that, as citizens of a peripheral Principality, they were and always would be politically expendable. Their peaceful demonstration, then, was undoubtedly laced with an unspoken threat: any more of this, and we normally not-very-political people might start looking at secession as a serious option.

Rather than take due note of this unprecedented display of disgruntlement, the nominally socialist PSC-PSOE, the main party in the Catalan government, chose to blame the whole thing on media manipulation of popular opinion. According to a widely publicised statement by an apparatchik-faced spokesperson called Joan Ferran, TV3 (the second most-watched channel in Catalonia) and Catalunya Ràdio (the most listened-to station) catered only to "nationalist minorities" and were "too critical" with the government. The names of certain politically suspect (albeit highly popular) broadcasters were mentioned. Well, I'm sure Comrade Joan knows what to do next: accuse them formally of crypto-separatist-deviationist tendencies, then purge them all from screen and dial for evermore. After all, it worked for the KGB. Come to think of it, it still does.

Our Nour

On the excellence of Barcelona-based band Nour's first album, *Papier Mullat*

Catalonia Today, 20 December 2007

This is a one hundred per cent, twenty-four carat recommendation for any readers still strapped for Christmas present ideas: go immediately, please— no dilly-dallying!—to your nearest record shop and request an album called *Papier Mullat* (sic) by a five-person band called Nour. Nour is the brain-child of Yacine Belahcene Benet, son of an Algerian father and a Catalan mother who grew up in the very same neighbourhood of Algiers that was blown to bits recently by some supposedly religious people. A few years after moving to Barcelona in 1993, Yacine founded *Cheb Balowski*, whose eleven members produced three albums and toured Europe, North Africa, and the Middle East with immense success before sheer weight of numbers led to their dissolution.

Although Nour was formed just a few months ago, it has already produced what is without a hint of a doubt one of the finest CDs to have come out of Catalonia this year. Yacine grew up quadrilingual, thus allowing him to mix his Catalan-language songs with liberal doses of Algerian Arabic, Spanish, and French (a full English translation is included in the sleeve notes) as natu-rally as all of Nour's musicians blend raï, rap, and rock. Any doubtful readers might take note that this album has nothing to do with those mercilessly half-baked sounds that rejoice, unblushing, in the name of World Music. On the contrary, *Papier Mullat* is musically brilliant, with lyrics as intelligent as they are down-to-earth. The first track alone—"Vida Moderna"—is worth the asking price: *Modern life for everyone/from other people's sweat/modern life for everyone/African sweat.* This got me, at least—advanced in age though I am—dancing myself into an appropriate lather.

Barfalona

On artist Enric Maurí's remarkable "anti-souvenirs"

Catalonia Today, 1 January 2008

Painter, singer, installationist, film-maker and photographer Enric Maurí (Cardedeu, 1957) has long railed against the simplistic overviews that visitors tend to have of Catalonia in general and, above all, of Barcelona. "The tourists don't see the real city," he says, "they just see Gaudí."

So he has decided to take his fight against cliché straight to these self-same tourists, by designing four Barcelona "souvenirs" that will be put on sale over the coming year: small figurines covered from head to toe in colourful *trencadís*, the trademark broken-up mosaic which Gaudí used to decorate the Parc Güell. The first of these figures is displayed crouching miserably in a cardboard street nest (a protest at the city's hallucinatorily high house prices). A second figure has an eternally clicking camera stuck to his face: a satirical take on the banality of the "cultural" tourism so much in vogue here. A third figure is poised in an artificially dynamic athletic pose, as a comment on the endless fanfaring of Barcelona as a once Olympic city. The real masterpiece, however, is the fourth and final figure in the series, who is bent drunkenly over, having just disgorged a pretty pool of Gaudiesque puke. This is the artist's sarcastic reminder that Barcelonan vomiters are legion: not only the plastered locals who redecorate the pavements on Sunday mornings, but also the foreigners who flock to the city in droves for their stag or hen nights, and end up splashing doorways yellow while dressed up in plastic breasts or penis-shaped hats. Just the kind of people, in fact, who will end up buying Maurí's chundering mosaic-skinned doll, as a permanent reminder of all the fun they had in the Catalan capital.

Just Say Nothing

On the covert hushing-up
of *La vida després de Déu [Life after God]*

Catalonia Today, 18 January 2008

Last Friday I was interviewed on the radio by Jordi García Soler, a journalist with 43 years of wide-ranging experience behind him. He decided to dedicate all 55 minutes of the talk to my latest book—an (informed) attack on organised religion called *La vida després de Déu [Life After God]*—because, according to him, "there have been serious attempts to silence it."

Hearing this from someone as much in the loop as García Soler, I finally realised that my gradually accumulated suspicions must have some foundation. True, a tiny handful of freelance authors and journalists have written about the book, motivated by personal conviction. But it is simply not normal that three months after publication—one of them spent on the best-seller lists—a book on an objectively controversial subject which is now going into a third edition, should not have received one single review anywhere at all in the Catalan Press (with the notable exception of *Catalonia Today*). One newspaper in a major Catalan city (not named, at the request of the journalist involved) even pulled a piece about the book at the last moment, to avoid offending a wealthy Catholic patron.

In short, most staff reviewers and commentators in this corner of Europe, presumably worried about possible repercussions, are avoiding *La vida després de Déu* as if it stank of skunk. My only consolation is that a far more famous book in a similar vein—Richard Dawkins's *The God Delusion*—has also been covertly sent to Coventry here, despite having caused massive splashes in just about every other country in the world: those happy lands whose Fourth Estates, far from cowering when the Church raises a finger to its lips, reply with an unambiguous finger gesture of their own.

Matthew Tree

Say What?

On a conservative Catalan politician's ridiculous poster campaign

Catalonia Today, 25 January 2008

Unió Democràtica de Catalunya (UDC), the most conservative of all the catalanocentric political parties, has been led for two decades by the lawyer Josep Antoni Duran i Lleida. The contrast of this Demochristian's intense defence of "family values" in public, with his rumoured fondness for (paid) ladies in private, long ago gave rise to the joke that Duran is Christian from the waist up and a democrat from the waist down. Thanks to his latest poster campaign we can now also say of him—this time with gossip-free certainty—that he is one lousy writer.

Take for example, his slogan concerning immigration: "People don't leave their country because they want to, but because they're hungry. But there isn't space for everybody in Catalonia." Right underneath this simplistic insinuation that every single member of Catalonia's million-strong foreign population is an undernourished desperado who has flooded into the country uninvited, lurks the all-purpose campaign adage: "They shall respect Catalonia," which reads here like a direct threat to any outsider who gets lippy. (In fact, *they* refers to the politicians in Madrid, but is so poorly contextualised that misunderstandings are inevitable.) To make matters worse, the whole is topped off by a striking image of Duran's follically-challenged, not-unMussolini-like head. For those self-confessed "non-nationalists" who are wont to accuse any support of things Catalan as xenophobic or even fascist, Duran's poster is manipulable manna from heaven. Before they start bad-mouthing, however, perhaps they should take into account that—his Catalanish rhetoric notwithstanding—Duran spends a fair percentage of his speeches attacking any move towards Catalan independence, almost certainly because his driving ambition is, and always has been, to become a minister in a Spanish government. One in which, presumably, there is space for absolutely anybody.

Temps Fora

On the launching of *Time Out Barcelona*

Catalonia Today, 2 February 2008

For well over a decade, different Catalan publishers have been coaxing, inveigling, and sweet-talking the owners of the London-based weekly *Time Out*, with a view to obtaining a franchise for a Barcelona edition. On January 10th of this year, the multimedia holding Cultura03 having won the bid, *Time Out Barcelona* appeared on the newsstands at long last, and promptly sold a healthy 25,000 copies. I don't think many Barcelonans would disagree that their city sorely needed a modern, all-embracing listings magazine (the perennial *Guía del Ocio*, incomplete and graphically unbearable, has never cut the mustard).

Time Out Barcelona shares most of the hallmarks of its London counterpart: a Gay and Lesbian section, a flurry of original tips for things to do in the city, regular columns by people who actually know how to write (Enric Gomà's deliriously droll television page alone is worth the cover price) and so on. However, there is one thing it thankfully doesn't have in common with *TO London* or its other English-language siblings: an inexplicable tendency on the part of the respective editors to place the most cringe-inducing puns imaginable at the head of every article. For example in the same week, *Time Out Abu Dhabi* announced a piece about golf with the words "Tee Time", *TO Sydney* reported on the city's "Bar Wars". *TO Israel* introduced a guide to 24-hour shops with the title "Clock Wise". Why oh why is such facetious flippancy inflicted on those magazines' hapless readers? Toni Puntí, the top banana at *TO Barcelona*, has successfully prevented such uncalled-for crassness from infecting his new magazine. Or, as the folk at the London edition might have put it: "Maiden Organ Says No To Pun Fun".

Najat

On Najat El Hachmi's winning of a prestigious Catalan-language literary award

Catalonia Today, 8 February 2008

A week ago today, Najat el Hachmi (Nador, Morocco, 1979) won the Rolls-Royce Phantom of Catalan-language literary awards: the Premi Ramon Llull, which comes steeped in prestige and decked out in 90,000 euros' worth of catch-free cash. Immediately—perhaps to disguise their lack of so much as a half-fingerprint of a clue as to who Najat El Hachmi was—most journalists covering the ceremony, spotting her North African roots, seized on a predictable buzzword beginning with the letter "I". Her as yet unpublished prize-winning novel, they averred, was about immigrants (it isn't), she herself was an example of how immigrants could be successfully integrated (an assertion she herself has disavowed), and so on and so forth.

Those of us who have known Najat for some time, by contrast, soon clocked her as that rare thing, a natural born writer. We had not only the evidence of her first book—a beautifully-written, cliché-smashing autobiography called *Jo també sóc catalana [I am Catalan, too]* (2004)—but also the woman herself, with her unfakeable seriousness about writing, her heartfelt recommendations of certain contemporary authors and biting write-offs of others and, above all, the way in which she, like all writers worthy of the name, can pass with equal enthusiasm from book-talk to all kinds of matters non-literary, proof positive she has steered clear of those ivory towers in which much of contemporary Catalan literature is still partially choking on the dust of academe. Najat El Hachmi, for us, is a shot in the arm, a gale of fresh air and a welcome addition to a future which, by the by, is looking up nicely. It is because of this, I suppose, that we find it so easy to clean forget she's an immigrant.

Sweet

On sweet fights and becoming an honorary cooper in Vilanova

Catalonia Today, 15 February 2008

Like many people I like my Sundays quiet, so when the singer Pere Tàpias invited me to see the carnivalesque *Batalla de Caramels* (Candy fight) in his home town of Vilanova i la Geltrú, and to become an honorary member of an odd-sounding *Confraria de Boters* (Brotherhood of Coopers), I tried to wriggle out of it. So engagingly insistent was he, however, that last Sunday morning but one saw me heading off to Vilanova, completely in the dark as to what I was letting myself in for.

No sooner had I arrived than Pere led me to the Plaça de la Vila and placed me on a balcony opposite the Town Hall. A moment later, fifteen banner-waving gangs of men and women of all ages, including a scattering of Africans and Moroccans, dressed in yellow, red, blue, and lilac *barretines* (Catalan hats) filled up the square below until it was seething with tension. Suddenly the PA system roared a cue, *La plaça és vostra! (The square is yours!)*, and they started to pelt each other with boiled sweets so vehemently it looked as if they were beating off predatory swarms of gnats. This fight over, the crowd, eight hundred strong, instantly formed twelve chorus lines across the square and performed a melodious, elegant, hokey-cokey-like song. Speechless after this display of colour, noise, music, and violence, I was taken to the peaceful, gardened Hotel César, fed a beautiful lunch, given a red and black morning coat and formally inducted into the Brotherhood of Coopers, by means of a curious ceremony involving wine and doggerel. And there was I thinking that Catalonia, bizarre country though it is, had no more surprises up its sleeve for me, not any more, not after 24 years of residence. Wrong again.

Matthew Tree

Not Quite a Fight

On a Mataronian African being improbably accused

Catalonia Today, 23 February 2008

Last Thursday evening, the tavern opposite the Mataró RENFE had the usual incongruous mix of people ever to be found in station bars: a smattering of sozzled old men, a lonely looking teenage girl, an odd couple (she a dyed blonde, he burly and greying, with an arm in plaster), a dapper African, myself, and Gary Gibson (an adoptive Mataronian and occasional contributor to this magazine, among other things).

Gary left, and, having time to kill, I was about to order another beer when the bouncer and the blonde started to scream insults at the African, claiming he had just pilfered their mobile. Offended, the African rapid-fired salvos of expletives back at his accusers. The barman, meanwhile, found the missing mobile in the toilet (either accidentally dropped or deliberately stashed, depending on whose version you believed).

The African now whipped out his defensive trump cards: he already owned a state-of-the-art cellphone (which he duly produced); he was an established citizen, having lived in Mataró for ten years; he was married to a Catalan woman (presumably to back up this assertion, he now started speaking in Catalan). But lurking behind his sound and fury was a thinly disguised amalgam of embarrassment and humiliation. After all, he was doubtless well aware that no matter how long he lived in Mataró, no matter how cutting-edge his gadgets, no matter how many Catalan wives he ended up going through, should he happen to fall under any suspicion, he would still forever have to prove himself by frantically brandishing these hard-won credentials in the air before an audience that would tend to assume they were phony. Being an African in Europe, it struck me as I passed his straining-to-be-proud face on the way out, was a full time job in itself.

Self-Sold Man

On an extraordinary self-publishing success

Catalonia Today, 3 March 2008

Joan Junyent used to be the managing director of a potash mine in Súria (near Manresa). An engineer specialising in accident prevention, he'd been working in the mining sector for over two decades. When, in August of 2004, his bosses slapped him in the face with a jumbo-sized wet fish by sacking him without notice, he turned for solace to what had, until then, been just a hobby: writing.

His then novel in progress was about accidents at work. Enlightened, perhaps, by the after-stun of his slap, it occurred to him to turn his book into a practical but highly readable quasi-manual. Thus was born *El gran silenci [The Big Silence]*, a curious cross between "a work of fiction and a basic course in accident prevention", as he puts it. He published it himself and immediately began peddling it to every kind of firm imaginable, from driving schools in Lleida to steel foundries in Euskadi.

The book has so far gone into nine editions and four languages, with total sales of nearly 25,000 copies, allowing Joan to pay off his mortgage and keep his family in clover, to boot. When he told me his story in the Súria public library a few weeks ago, I practically head-butted the wall in frustration. This man had successfully avoided all the infuriating drawbacks of the book world: the endless waits for publisher's decisions, the fickleness of the literary prize-giving circuit, the maddening blunders of the distributors and the soul-destroying put-downs of the critics. Joan wanted to buy me lunch, but I insisted that I pick up the tab, by way of congratulating him for having unwittingly—and unerringly—made a laughingstock of all those writers who like to think of ourselves as "professional".

Matthew Tree

Lit Up

On the emergence of a
new literary genre based on booze

Catalonia Today, 6 March 2008

Years and years ago, Jan Vardoen (any, if there are any, fanatical followers of this column will remember him from a piece published in March of 2006, as the chef turned printer turned boat-builder turned cocktail barman turned major Norwegian singer-songwriter) told me about an author called Jeffrey Bernard, described by Jan as the English Charles Bukowski.

Los Angeles-born Bukowski (1920-1994) dedicated king-sized chunks of his mainly autobiographical prose to the drawbacks and blessings of being a full-time alcoholic. Booze, in all its motley forms, gatecrashes the action of his novels so often you could be forgiven for thinking it was the star guest. Jeffrey Bernard, who I read only recently, is uncannily similar in both style and content: short, careful sentences not unlike those of a lush trying to cover up a slur, and an ironic insistence on the author's penchant for spirit-fuelled self-destruction. It struck me that maybe these two writers had unwittingly started a new genre: *Alco Lit*, meaning not books written by writers who happen to be alcoholics—in that case, it'd be the largest literary genre in the world—but narratives in which the hard stuff is an essential ingredient. I mention all this partly because a handful of people—that is to say, all of my readers—have pointed out that alcohol features prominently (excessively, even) in my own books. I for one, though, am positive that I don't deserve to join the ranks formed by Bernard and Bukowski. For one thing, I never write when drunk. Although, now I think about it, I often do write with a hangover the size of a haystack. As may or may not be noticeable in the article you've just read.

Flaming Amis

On the work of Martin Amis

Catalonia Today, 15 March 2008

It was with a kind of irritated curiosity that, two issues back, I read Joseph Wilson's piece in *Catalonia Today* about Martin Amis, whose novel *House of Meetings* has just appeared in Catalan and Spanish, and whose collection of essays *The Second Plane* was published in Britain last week.

"Irritated curiosity", because Amis is a writer I've never trusted, without understanding exactly why. Even in his supposedly good novels, such as *Money* (1986), I've always suspected him of holding something back, too busy with the window-dressing to deliver the goods, so to speak. This suspicion was reinforced by *Experience* (2000), an autobiography which reveals nothing whatsoever about its author except how skilled he is at doing precisely that.

Worse still is Amis's more recent tendency to pontificate on Stalinism and, especially, Islam, which—as Wilson's article showed—has led him to make a series of generalisations as steeped in solemnity as they are manifestly silly. It wasn't, however, until critic Emili Manzano interviewed Amis last week on Canal 33, that this much-revered novelist finally flashed his Achilles' heel in a single sentence: "Being a writer involves three things: the writing itself, the reading, and, of course, a little living, too." Ironic though he was trying to be, he had, it seemed to me, unwittingly exposed his work as a contrived web, word-spun out of a lettered, monied, and relatively un-driven life ("a little living"). Nothing but piss and wind, in harder words, like the English private schoolboys I used to know so well and have tried all my life to forget, and whose ghastly pseudo-wisdom Amis—ensconced before the cameras and holding forth to the manner born—reminded me of so hauntingly.

Matthew Tree

Catchwords
On a possible nightmare scenario
Catalonia Today, 22 March 2008

Last Friday a friend told me how he and three other Catalans had been asked to leave a restaurant in Valladolid for linguistic reasons: *Si queréis hablar en catalán, mejor lo hacéis en otro sitio (If you want to speak in Catalan, go do it somewhere else)* were the manager's exact words. It was no coincidence that this little contretemps took place in 2004, the year when the negotiation process for the new Catalan Statute of Autonomy got into its stride, thus spurring certain Spanish journalists—notably those working for *El Mundo* newspaper and the bishop-financed COPE radio station—to feed outrageous pork pies to their audiences, in their eagerness to block said Statute by portraying the Catalans as a treacherous, grasping, alien people. From then on, reported cases of Catalan-baiting have increased over the years. In 2005, a Barcelona taxi driver had to leave Saragossa in a hurry before his yellow and black cab was stoned. In 2006, a teenage girl was physically threatened on the Madrid metro for speaking in Catalan to a friend. And so on and so forth.

In a recent book on the post-Bosnian-war Hague trials, Croatian novelist Slavenka Drakulic stresses the importance of the odium built up for a decade before the conflict by the Croatian and Serbian media. Without it, she states categorically, there would have been no fighting, let alone the countless rapes, tortures, and murders that went with it. Using Drakulic's calculations as a rule of thumb and taking 2004 as our starting point, we have just six more years of anti-Catalan spin to go before venomous words turn into deeds, and the first tanks start to rumble down the Diagonal. The fateful annum? That for which several groups in the Catalan parliament have already proposed a referendum for independence: 2014.

Shop 'Til You Droop

On the very depressing atmosphere
to be found in major shopping centres

Catalonia Today, 29 March 2008

Last Saturday, for the first time ever I spent more than fifteen minutes in a large shopping centre. It happened to be the Centre Comercial Glòries on Barcelona's Avinguda Diagonal, but could have been any one of the countless complexes dedicated to hard-core purchasing to be found in just about every corner of Catalonia.

I lasted three whole hours. Like anyone else, I have to shop from time to time, and like anyone else, I sometimes find it easier to do so in a place that sells anything from children's shoes to pork fillet—to name two items on my shopping list—in a relatively confined space. So why, just moments after entering this space, did I feel so lousy, so down in the mouth, so in need of five shots of tequila? Perhaps it was the war-memorial-sized, disarmingly expressionless inflatable rabbit of welcome in the foyer. Perhaps it was the hangar dimensions of the Carrefour supermarket, along whose tiring aisles I searched in vain for noodles to go with the pork. Perhaps it was the slowness of the escalators carrying laden shoppers to their next port of call, their faces grim with patience. Or, who knows?, maybe it was the frankfurt-and-coffee odour of the numerous snack bars, their internal terraces trapped under poor lighting, a vapid puff of buy-talk rising in flatulent bursts from their many customers. Whatever. By the time I got out of there I felt as if my brain had been erased, that life had even less meaning than usual, that the sky would remain forever grey. The following day, as if the C.C. Glòries itself was trying to justify my gloom, I discovered the pork bought there was four days past its sell-by date and smelt of wasted time.

Matthew Tree

Eventless

On the most depressing book presentation
I've ever given
Catalonia Today, 5 April 2008

Last Friday I went to one of the smallest towns on the Maresme coast, invited by a cultural organiser there to present my latest book. At the last minute he told me he hadn't ordered any copies, but luckily the publishers managed to courier me a baker's dozen in time for me to lug them onto the train.

The organiser picked me up from the station and, by chance, we ran into three friends of his who followed us into the venue: a huge, unlit house the outside and inside of which were conspicuously free of any indication a book was going to be presented there. (The organiser explained it had been impossible to print any posters "because of Holy Week"). Twenty minutes past the appointed time, it was clear that not a single soul was going to turn up. He suggested we went to a bar, on the way to which he told his friends—not me—that he'd been experimenting with a new poster design, and pulled out a wad of placards on which, I noticed with surprise, news of my presentation was prominently displayed. When I asked him why he hadn't put any of these things up, he shrugged, smiling: "bad organisation".

In the bar, I asked when it would be convenient for him to give me a (previously agreed) lift back to Barcelona. He replied that as there hadn't been a presentation, I could now catch the train. Mercifully, one of his friends offered to drive me and my bagful of superfluous books back to the real world, far from this tiny coastal Twilight Zone to which writers were summoned for the sole purpose, as far as I could see, of being politely humiliated until it dawned on them just how very expendable they were.

Game Not Over

On a benefit concert for the
Grup d'Afectats d'Esclerosi Múltiple

Catalonia Today, 16 April 2008

Last Thursday, the Grup d'Afectats d'Esclerosi Múltiple (GAEM) organised their first live concert—*Esclerock*—with a view to raising funds for an international research project underway in a Badalona hospital, which aims to develop a definitive cure for certain forms of multiple sclerosis by 2010. From the wings I watched Quimi Portet, Miqui Puig, Mazoni, and Nour take an audience in the Palau de la Música's smaller auditorium from surreal love songs through to a finale which had even the back rows leaping to their feet and the two founders of the GAEM beating out the time from wheelchairs propelled enthusiastically onto centre-stage.

I used to teach English to one of them, back in the days when mobile phones looked like loaves of bread and most people believed CD-ROMs would end up replacing books. I lost touch with her for years until we ran into each other by the quietest of chance in a Barcelona market last year. When I fatuously asked her how she was, she gestured wearily at her wheelchair and told me about her diagnosis.

There are 6000 MS sufferers in Catalonia, 40,000 in the whole of Spain and some two and a half million worldwide. Not enough, it seems, to make it worth the pharmaceutical companies' while to invest one of their many mountains of cash in a search for a serious remedy, as opposed to merely palliative treatments. So a small group of affected people in a small corner of Europe have decided that this particular buck stops with them. The concert netted a satisfying 15,000 euros worth of pure research money—all the musicians and technicians having volunteered their skills for free—and the time flew by because we were enjoying ourselves. Please feel free to do as you see fit: *www.gaem-bcn.org*.

Matthew Tree

Weird Doings

On a strange series of encounters, one afternoon in London

Catalonia Today, 17 April 2008

2pm, last Saturday, next to Victoria station, London. My friend Max and I had just met up with a view to talking the hind leg off the afternoon, but no sooner had we opened our mouths than we were buttonholed by an elderly lady whose upmarket voice declared that she could not abide girls who wore jeans then pointed at several who happened to be passing and huffed, "Look at those bottoms, how absolutely disgusting!"

Chuckling nervously at her quirkiness, Max and I sought refuge in an empty pub but when I came back to our table with the drinks Max had been joined by an elderly man in a wheelchair with an outsize woolly hat on his head who launched into a tirade about how the Twin Towers had been primed with explosives by the CIA then shifted to how he had almost been killed by an infection of the brain before pulling off his hat to reveal that a third of his cranium had been surgically removed. Hungry, we left for lunch, laughing at the coincidence of running into two (fairly) weird, old strangers in the space of an hour.

In the restaurant, Max, taken aback by the waitress's undeniable beauty, asked her where she was from and was told to guess which we did wrongly a dozen times until she impatiently informed us she was from Portugal at which point I blurted out some nonsense in pidgin Portuguese while Max showered her with heaven only knows what compliments, both of us tee-heeing a touch hysterically due to the booze and the strange afternoon and now our social clumsiness in front of this young woman in whose increasingly wary eyes we had clearly turned into two (fairly) weird, old strangers. Our sails abruptly bereft of wind, we paid the bill and hastened our bejeaned bottoms out into the incipient rain.

Calling a Turd a Turd

On toilets, Oxford, bureaucracy
and excrement generally

Catalonia Today, 27 April 2008

When Francesc and Rosario, psychologists both, decided to take a year's sabbatical from Barcelona to do research at Oxford University, I immediately repeated after Amy Winehouse, "No, no, no, no!", clarifying that at OU they would be surrounded by hordes of elite-obsessed, puffed up people of all ages who were unable to laugh without sniggering superciliously and unable to speak without circumlocuting like inebriated aristocrats from another century, in a setting of biscuit-coloured towers lined with stone pustules topping fridge-temperature buildings maintained by underpaid Maltese flunkeys. They went anyway.

Since then, Francesc—while not finding the place in itself that bad—has become increasingly frustrated at the way his Oxford colleagues snootily keep him at arm's length, making it difficult for him to work with them efficiently. He recently gave me an extreme example of what he's up against. Noticing that the lab wing's toilet was practically engulfed in excrement both fresh and stale, he informed the department through the intranet, "The gents facilities are flooding and smell funny!" Their (first) reply, "Either your message will be posted to the [intranet] list or you will receive notification of the moderator's decision." Which decision finally came through two days later: *Posting of your message has been rejected by the moderator. The moderator gave the following reason for rejecting your request: "Your message was deemed inappropriate by the moderator".* Even as you read this a full week later, the toilet in question is still sitting complacently in its own stench, which strikes me as a perfect metaphor for Oxford University itself, my loathing of whose foul and pompous imperturbability dates from the very first day I arrived—in the guise of an aspiring student—in what the poet Matthew Arnold inexplicably dubbed "that sweet city with her dreaming spires".

Lifting the Lid

On meeting the remarkable daughter
of a remarkable man

Catalonia Today, 6 May 2008

We got talking in the departure lounge, the little old lady and I, last Thursday evening, both of us on our way to Cork. Once on board, we discovered that Aer Lingus—which numbers its seats—had coincidentally placed us next to each other.

On discovering I was from England, she mentioned her father had spent several years there after the war and it was a short step from there to her telling the (astounding) story of this unaccountably little-known man.

Constantí Llambias (Barcelona, 1898) was a heart and lung specialist who came up with a unique scheme to allow blind people to gain a livelihood by running their own lottery. Founded in 1934 by Llambias and his partner Roc Boronat, the Sindicat de Cecs de Catalunya (SCC) sold a thousand tickets in its first two years. Franco and his minions, on hearing of the success of Llambias's brainchild, abducted it to create the Organización Nacional de Ciegos de España—the now omnipresent ONCE—while banning the SCC, forcing Llambias into ten years of exile, raiding his Barcelona home then absconding with his medical records and other documents to Salamanca, where they remain. So successfully was he wiped off the official slate that as late as 1992, the ONCE display at the Seville Expo could claim without batting an eyelid that the idea for a sightless persons' sweepstake had originated in Burgos in 1938. My thanks, then, to Llambias's septuagenarian yet crystal-clear-headed daughter Montserrat for having thrown a little light on recent Catalan history, whose contributions to the world we generally seem to be kept in the dark about, unless by the slightest of chances we find ourselves on the right plane with the right little old lady.

Unforgettable

On the rampant cultural fraud committed in so many Catalan coastal resorts

Catalonia Today, 9 May 2008

Given time, most of us get used to the fact that there are whole swathes of coastal Catalonia which tourists can visit safe in the knowledge that not a single bacillus of the surrounding culture stands a chance of penetrating the contrived vacuum in which they willingly while away their holidays. So it is that in places like Santa Susanna or Platja d'Aro you can walk yourself weary trying to find a local newspaper, say, or a plate of esqueixada (but can pick up a horned bottle of sangría or a plastic flamenco dancer in the twinkling of an eye).

It was in Santa Susanna, in fact, that I spent last weekend, and was surprised to stumble across a general store that was atypical for the area, being upmarket and tat-free and clearly aimed at what a snob would call the discerning customer. Curious to see if they also sold a different class of souvenir here, I soon discovered that—like everywhere else—all the available mementoes were emblazoned with the word *España* and the visual clichés that tend to accompany it. True, these relatively costly items had "original" designs. For instance, Osbourne-type bulls covered in Gaudí-style mosaic. But that didn't change the fact that anything that so much as reeked of Catalanness had been carefully camouflaged, even if it meant mating a non-Spanish-speaking Catalan architect with Spain's national beast. What price the numerous public initiatives to promote Catalonia abroad if even in the "smart" souvenir shops along the Catalan coast, tourists are still being fed the old fascist lie that Spain is all one and the same, from Santa Susanna to San Sebastián? The shopkeepers themselves, of course, justify such cultural perjury by claiming that foreign visitors are oblivious to the reality of Catalonia, conveniently forgetting that reality, to paraphrase a sage phrase, begins at home.

Franki Goes to Can Brians

On the absurd punishment meted out
to alleged flag-tugger Francesc Argemí

Catalonia Today, 16 May 2008

Francesc Argemí (*Franki* to his friends) is a 28 year old man from Terrassa who, back in 2002, apparently tried to tug a Spanish flag off the balcony of that city's city council. Last week, he was sentenced to two years and seven months of hard porridge for insulting Spain and disturbing the peace. This kind of nationalistic overkill—inconceivable though it is in all other countries excepting China, Turkey, Russia, and little Serbia—is beginning not to be news anymore.

For twenty odd years, young Catalans have been banged up at increasingly frequent intervals for casting aspersions on symbols of Spanish nationhood, for which those in power apparently wish to enforce a quasi-religious reverence. In 1988, for example, the 18-year-old independentist Núria Cadenas, from Barcelona, was put away for five years on trumped-up terrorist charges. In 2004, the Lloret de Mar home of 14-year-old linguistic militant Èric Bertran was raided by 20 heavily-armed Civil Guards who promptly accused him, too, of terrorism and carted him off to Madrid, unaware that the Army of the Phoenix which he claimed to lead was a fictional creation by J.K. Rowling. In 2007, 30-year-old Jaume Roura from Banyoles was also given a one-way ticket to the Spanish capital for burning a photograph of the Spanish King.

Franki Argemí, then, is simply the latest in a long line of groundlessly fingered Catalan activists. I mention all this not just to pass the time, but for the benefit of the many consulates in Barcelona which, I have been reliably informed, glean their Catalan news from this very paper. Perhaps they might feel the need to inform their respective governments about how freedom of expression—insisted upon by Article 11 of the European Union's Charter of Fundamental Rights—is being respected in Catalonia today?

On Hold

On a centre for people
with neurological illnesses

Catalonia Today, 22 May 2008

Not only prisons keep their portals locked. The Associació Vallès Amics de la Neurologia (AVAN), like many other voluntary organisations dedicated to the care of people with damaged nervous systems, ensures that the gates of its centre in Sabadell are secured at all times to prevent its patients from drifting into a world that doesn't have a clue as to their particular needs and difficulties.

When I went there last week, I was expecting to see mainly middle-aged or elderly people, more likely as they were to be affected by Parkinson's, MS, Attention Deficit Disorder, and similar illnesses. So it was a surprise to find a very young man in the audience. It turned out he'd been in a car crash, then six months of coma, and now he was fighting to make the simplest moves, to mouth the shortest of syllables.

But what impressed me most was not just the sight of him bravely going through his as yet limited motions, but a sudden flash of a feeling that I'd somehow known—and known well—his pre-crash self, so familiar did the healthy, amiable, outgoing 22-year-old lurking in his immobile eyes seem to me. It was as if I'd just recognised a friend.

No wonder, I realised, that recently I've been getting more involved with what used to be called charities that help what used to be called handicapped people. I don't do it for the warm afterglow that some do-gooders claim as compensation for their work. Given that I am ever more aware that absolutely anyone at any time might be condemned by illness or accident to a wheelchair or a zimmer frame and find themselves requiring the services of associations like the AVAN, I do it selfishly bearing everyone I care about in mind. Myself above all.

Matthew Tree

Losing the Game

On the reasons for the author's complete lack of interest in football and all other sports

Catalonia Today, 21 June 2008

Last Thursday there was an end-of-term soccer match at my children's primary school. The older players (aged six) really got into the spirit of the thing, dribbling, crying foul, and scoring goals with an almost professional sternness. However, most of the younger players (aged five), although they ran about a bit and dutifully tried to tap the spheroid when it rolled their way, clearly didn't see the point of the exercise, presumably because key concepts such as "my team" or "winning" were not (yet) in their vocabulary.

My heart went out to them as certain long buried memories of mine suddenly rose from their tombs. All through my school days, I was unable to understand either the why or the wherefore of competitive sports. The very idea of joining up with a group to symbolically "beat" other people by kicking (or throwing) a ball struck me—and strikes me still—as uninteresting at best, and, at worst, plain misguided. I have just never got it, any more than I have got, say, moth collecting or cribbage. So it is that I have lived a life free of the thrills—visibly real for the majority, including most of my friends—of football (or any other sport).

This foregoing has never given me any grief, except on those occasional occasions when Catalan acquaintances—having discovered that I don't follow football despite being English—manifest as much astonishment as if I'd just sprouted a third ear. To clarify matters, I usually explain that football in England is a bit like drinking there. You either consume near-fatal quantities or you abstain altogether. I chose to abstain from the former, if not from the latter. Then again, I add pointedly, when it comes to a choice between drinking and football, there's simply no competition.

Shut It

On some recent cases of censorship

Catalonia Today, 30 June 2008

The first magazine to suppress an article of mine was an anarchist weekly and it took me by nasty surprise because at the time—1985—this magazine, *Black Flag*, was the only one in the world that was publishing anything by me at all. The article—about the potential role of the different nationalities of the USSR in a post-Soviet future—was rejected on the grounds that the subject was nationalistic (and therefore unanarchist).

Years passed before another article was censored, this time in Catalonia by *El Punt*, who deemed it in poor taste—being as it was about the law against images of erect penises in pre-Internet Britain—despite the fact that the same newspaper had enthusiastically received several previous articles of mine about porn, smut, and filth generally. Yet more unexpected was the suppression of a single word in a microsketch I wrote for Andreu Buenafuentes's 1997 series *La cosa nostra*. The word *vulva* was vetoed as too crude and replaced with the apparently more genteel *vagina*.

Only last week, I was astonished when—not wanting to lose any advertising revenue—a well-known Catalan newspaper rejected a column that took a tiny bit of mickey out of a well-known Catalan bank. Even that was as nothing compared to what had happened the previous day, when I hosted a prize-giving ceremony for Catalan school students. I had asked my presenter to mention the title—just the title!—of my latest book (which questions the validity of organised religion). The powers in charge instructed her not to do so because *there would be representatives of Christian schools attending who might be offended.* Which statement immediately brought to mind the once controversial playwright Joe Orton's description of all such nit-picking bowdlerizers: *Too nervous to live.*

Matthew Tree

Oh Ay

On the nasty things that happened here
after the Spanish squad's European victory

Catalonia Today, 19 July 2008

It's a bit late in the day to talk about the Catalan aftermath of the Spanish squad's skilful winning of the European Championship at the end of June. Only now, however, have certain post-match incidents come to light, all of them involving that minority of Catalans still under the posthumous, yet lingering spell of Francisco Franco Bahamonde. When Spain won the semi-finals, some of these youths were already cruising round Barcelona's well-heeled Sant Gervasi district in Mummy's car screaming "Catalanes, hijos de puta!".

But that was nothing compared to what happened after the victory itself, as related by Vicent Partal (founder of *Vilaweb*, the first online newspaper in Spain). In Vic, a journalist from the local paper was collared by Spain fans and forced at fist-point to shout "Viva España"; in Barcelona, a Moroccan was beaten up on the Rambla for being "unworthy" of waving a Spanish flag; in Reus, Catalan flags were burnt wholesale by Spain fans giving the Roman salute; all over the country, interactive Catalan-language websites were flooded with hate messages and death threats.

On a grander scale, the usual Catalan-taunting in certain Spanish media was immediately jacked up to a fever pitch in part thanks to a much-boosted manifesto signed by a baker's dozen and a half of pro-Castilian intellectuals that reads like an incitement to linguistic—if not ethnic—cleansing. And Spain won, for heaven's sake! Can anyone imagine what would have happened if they'd lost? Or—heaven help us—if the winner had been a finally legalised Catalan squad? Ever since 1976, politicians and sports people both Spanish and Catalan have frequently and prissily pontificated that sports should not be mixed with politics, apparently oblivious to the obvious: in the half-baked state currently called the Kingdom of Spain, sport is politics.

Dawning of the Age

On being told to stop drinking even beer
all summer long

Catalonia Today, 24 July 2008

As Old Bastard Time takes his toll, you learn to dread visiting the doctor, given that for every illness you own up to he'll almost certainly discover a brace more. So it was that having cured a stomach problem, my GP discovered my cholesterol was peaking and my liver was a touch inflamed. I didn't mind being put on a diet that would have depressed a fruitarian, but balked at the executive order not to touch any alcohol for the entire summer, no, not so much as a freezer-chilled beer served in a glass opaque with frost under the sultry Barcelonan sky.

Now, an alcoholic I am not. This I know because way back when, I was checked into a psychiatric hospital many of whose patients were bona fide dipsomaniacs whose confessions have kept the living daylights scared out of me to this day. But I do enjoy a beer or five, especially when the ups and downs of work leave my brain feeling like a trodden-on biscuit.

That notwithstanding, I clambered obediently onto the wagon, replacing beer with soft drinks (above all the insipid squash ambitiously called Aquarius). After just eight days I was tired, wired, and bloated with cheap pop. I realised that without beer, I was going to get very sick indeed. I duly cracked a few, enjoying every aspect of the little beauties, from their discreet fizz through to the blissful way they massaged my tauter thoughts. Duly healed, the following Sunday I hoisted myself back onto the wagon and I am riding in it still and will continue to do so throughout the summer, much as the doctor ordered. After all, any desert can be crossed if it has a few oases— liquid first-aid kits, so to speak—lurking here and there.

Matthew Tree

Hair Yesterday

On a book revealing the contribution
to the Holocaust made by the
cosmetics multinational L'Oréal

Catalonia Today, 31 July 2008

If an English copy of Monica Waitzfelder's true story *L'Oréal Took My Home* hadn't been slipped to me recently by the translator, Peter Bush, I would never (ever) have come across this remarkably ugly case of hypocrisy, dishonesty, and historical whitewashing on the part of the largest cosmetics multinational in the world (whose advertising clout is largely responsible for the media vacuum in which Waitzfelder's book has been screaming unheard since 2004).

Put briefly: the post-war HQ of L'Oréal Deutschland was purchased from a pro-Nazi insurance company which, back in 1938, had obliged the original owner—Monica's German-Jewish grandfather—to sign away his home to ensure his family's safety. (To little avail: he died in 1945 from illnesses contracted in French internment camps and his wife Kaethe was gassed in Auschwitz. Only his daughter Edith, Monica's mother, survived the war.)

For sixty years, L'Oréal has used a comprehensive range of subterfuges to hide the fact that their German operation was housed in property stolen from murdered people whose rightful heirs the company knew full well were still alive. What is worse, such discrimination is not, perhaps, a mere coincidence: the founder of L'Oréal, Eugène Schueller, bankrolled the French fascist organisation La Cagoule, whose thugs blew up synagogues and collaborated tongue-to-arse with the Nazis during the Occupation, before joining Schueller on L'Oréal's board of directors after the war. Worse still, his son-in-law André Bettencourt started his professional life as a pathologically anti-semitic pamphleteer and the latter's widow Liliane B., remains the largest individual shareholder in L'Oréal: an enterprise as boycottable as any other whose holdings include Cacherel, Lancôme, and a well-known UK firm called—with unconscious macabreness, given L'Oréal still refuses to cough up compensation for its specific contribution to the Shoah—The Body Shop.

Small Train Coming

On a miniature train circuit in Barcelona

Catalonia Today, 7 August 2008

Not too many people know about Barcelona's Parc de l'Oreneta and indeed neither did I until tipped off by my own family one recent Sunday. The park's steepish slopes north of the Sarrià district include a donkey sanctuary, a chicken restaurant and, at the very top, a miniature railway circuit, complete with a downsized station, old-fashioned cardboard tickets, hand-built steam locomotives and a route that leads through the narrowest of tunnels, around compact bends, over brief bridges and back into the station after a change of tiny little points.

As far as I know, Catalonia has only two other similar circuits, in Cornellà and Sabadell respectively. I've been on all of them and will go on all of them again, partly because the steam flow reminds me of my frequent train trips to Liverpool when I was five or so in the early 1960s but mainly because sitting in a dwarf railway carriage makes me feel like a child, period. I even played a minor role in the setting up of the Sabadell track. When the City Council (rightly) suspected that the (English) suppliers of the rolling stock were deliberately short-changing them, I was hired as an interpreter and joined a Council representative on the next plane out to Manchester. After hours of tough haggling we managed to save the Sabadell ratepayer a bunch of money and flew back the next morning so full of job-well-done glow that when the hostess offered us free champagne at just half past ten we nodded yes and got euphorically tipsy in the a.m. sunlight as the plane began its blue-windowed seaward approach to Barcelona. It was one of those inconsequentially blissful moments that nevertheless are never forgotten: almost as good as riding on a miniature train.

Brushed Off

On being rejected for reasons
of home decorating

Catalonia Today, 14 August 2008

After my last snooty rejection by a UK publisher—which I described in this column with overstudied nonchalance in early 2007—I swore I would never again submit a sentence more to that Island Nation. However, as Robert Burns concisely put it, "The best laid schemes o' mice an' men/Gang aft agley."

Recently I heard of a small press in Nottingham that not only published work by little-known writers—and in Britain I am nothing if not little-known—but was also specifically interested in authors from or based in Catalonia. At last, I thought, someone who knows the score and won't consider me a crank—or, as several people have done without any apparent comic intent, a crafty opportunist—for writing in Catalan as well as English. Tossing cynicism to the winds, I sent off my two unpublished books in English (including *Calling Card*, now being serialised in this paper) as well as a selection of articles. I got a fast reply from the publisher, who started off friendly, saying he'd enjoyed the articles but didn't think they'd sell. Fair enough!, I consoled myself. When it came to the books, however, he explained that his upcoming list was full and made a point of adding that he wouldn't be extending it in the near future because he was pressed for time due to a leaking window in his front room and a host of other DIY-related bits and bobs. Blow me, I thought, as I re-read his message, how many writers can there be who have been rejected for reasons of home decorating? Should anyone reading this have had a similar experience, please don't bother writing in to tell me about it: there's a mirror needs hanging on my wall.

Dear Oh Dear

On how tourism is making Barcelona both dearer and tackier

Catalonia Today, 7 September 2008

Last week, *Catalonia Today*'s Marion Cadier asked half a dozen tourists for their views of the Catalan capital and got much the same answers from all: lots to do, friendly locals, heaps of Gaudí. Had a thousand been interviewed, they wouldn't have come up with anything more perspicacious, even if Marion had threatened to whack it out of them with copies of the *Rough Guide* in the crypt of the Sagrada Família.

Sightseers everywhere are famous for their powerlessness of observation. Odd, though, that the interviewees didn't mention the city's expensiveness (it is the 20th priciest metropolis on the planet, beating Berlin, Madrid and even Moscow). Little could they guess that before tourists began to choose Barcelona for their holidays—as opposed to the Catalan beach resorts—any citizen on the then equivalent of a modest salary could live the nightlife of Riley and eat out at least once a week to boot.

Since then, bar and restaurant owners have taken to celebrating the presence of hordes of transient spenders by charging a lot more for a lot less. Take Can Ros in the Barceloneta neighbourhood, for instance, once a friendly, reasonably-priced seafood restaurant. When I went there recently, I was served an over-oily and only partly identifiable fish that cost its weight in saffron by Catalan waiters who had been trained to snap at the mainly foreign clientèle in an English broken beyond the use of superglue.

I ruefully stared at a copy of the *Barcelona Time Out City Guide* lying on a busy nearby table. The first person to include Can Ros in that book had been myself, years ago, when, desperate to keep the job, I had tried to impress the editors by including places frequented exclusively by discerning locals.

Pocket Pickings

On what it's like to have the tax people
extort a small fortune from you

Catalonia Today, 7 September 2008

In the year of our Lord 2005, I earned 5,000 euros from a company that for some reason never sent me an invoice to confirm the payment. Three years later, the Spanish Inland Revenue (called *Hisenda*, and other words, in Catalan) discovered I hadn't declared those 5,000 euros (not having had the invoices to hand) and instantly insisted that I not only pay the tax due, but also accumulated interest and assorted fines to a total tune of—what a coincidence—5,000 euros. An easy enough oversight has just put me in debt for the next two years.

I can't even console myself by imagining I've involuntarily done my mite towards improving the state of the local hospitals and schools, given that Catalonia surrenders nearly 10% of its income tax to central government: too much to allow serious investment in its own public services. With the exception, it then struck me, of the Catalan police. The Mossos d'Esquadra get more expensively equipped with each year that passes. So much so, indeed, that when a Swiss food critic disappeared this June after doing a runner from the El Bulli restaurant in Roses, the Mossos didn't hesitate to jump into a costly helicopter and, fearing the worst, scoured the area in search of his corpse (which they didn't find, the critic having absconded to Geneva, alive and gobbling). Last week, the cost of this futile operation was revealed to be—as you might have guessed—exactly 5,000 euros. The money has to come from somewhere and I wouldn't be at all surprised if it's coming from me. If so, I hope those policemen enjoyed their ride. And that a certain Swiss gourmet chokes to within an inch of his life over his next three rosette meal.

Crying Shame

On the British role in the Bosnian War

Catalonia Today, 7 September 2008

It was with mixed feelings that I finally saw Radovan Karadzic sitting in the Hague dock. Not because it had taken so long to place him there (indeed, European justice has been relatively swift with this particular war criminal: 85% of the 8,000 active employees at Auschwitz, for example, never even saw the inside of a courthouse) but because the sight of him brought back the frustration of reading about Bosnian civilians being burned alive, raped en masse, bombed and snipered to death in their own capital or massacred in farm sheds, while the (mainly British) negotiators dilly-dallied their way through all this bloodshed with less firmness of purpose than if dealing with a conflict over fishing rights.

A slew of recent books—among them, Daniele Conversi's *The Disintegration of Yugoslavia*—have provided a credible explanation for this dithering. In 1992, Serbian president Slobodan Milosevic, having been foiled in his attempts to dominate Yugoslavia by Germany's prompt recognition of Slovenian and Croatian independence, opted for an ethnocentric Greater Serbia for which he annexed whole swathes of Bosnia through his dead-keen proxy, Karadzic. Britain, opposed on principle to Bosnian secession and wanting to counteract what it perceived as excessive Teutonic influence in the Balkans, took over the "peace" process, blockaded arm sales to all sides (a move which weakened only the Bosnians), and then did its level best to play down the butchering of some 32,000 Bosnian civilians while trying to accommodate the Serb perpetrators, whom it wished to emerge as both winners and allies. No wonder the now universally vilified Karadzic— whose official wartime spokesman, the English academic John Zametica, had strongly influenced the Foreign Office's Bosnian policy—has the beady, vengeful look of someone just itching to blow his whistle.

Matthew Tree

That's Entertainment

On the large number of London musicals based on hackneyed old films

Catalonia Today, 12 September 2008

You don't have to be Max Planck to guess that recurrent visits to the same place will result in the repetition of certain familiar experiences. Yet in all the years that I've been popping back to London, I'd never noticed until this summer to what extent the musicals playing in that city's West End were an open invitation for ex-citizens such as myself to gorge themselves on a feast of déjà vu, given that just about all of them were based on old feature films that rang bell after irritating bell. The stage version of *Billy Elliott*, for example—adapted from a decade-old upbeat weepie about a twinkle-toed miner's son—was filling its house night after night, as were similar adaptations of *Hairspray* and the hoary old *Lion King* and even *Dirty Dancing* (once so outré and now downright passé).

The posters advertising these spectaculars—with their shots of performers stretching out their arms in limited ecstasy and haloed in Press flattery ("Best show in town", "Funniest show in town" etc.)—guaranteed so much sure-fire, above-board fun that I began to wonder if there was something wrong with me for finding them not only off-putting but downright creepy, as if I was being confronted by a cluster of the blockbuster undead (prising open their dusty movie cans with yesterday's songs on bony grins). I'm as nostalgic as the next middle-aged man, but not for all the beer in the Czech Republic was I going to be a party to this bloodless resuscitation of a part of the soundtrack of the past. It's not that I have any objection to taking the occasional trip down memory lane, I just really, really don't feel like making a song and dance about it.

Yakkety Yak

On Hugo Chávez, Sarah Palin, and other politicians
who play on local fears

Catalonia Today, 21 September 2008

By coincidence, the other day the news channel 3/24 followed up an item on the loudmouthed US vice-presidential nominee Sarah Palin with one on the equally loudmouthed Venezuelan president Hugo Chávez, thus unexpectedly revealing them to be (cosmetic differences notwithstanding) the spitting images of each other.

Palin outspokenly opposed abortion (even for rape victims) while supporting the gun lobby to the hilt, in the presumable belief that people have the right to make it out of even the most reluctant womb so as to be shot at with impunity. Chávez, for his part, was shown bawling his head off about an apparent American plot against his regime for which there is so little evidence he can't even charge his own suspects.

According to the Slovene thinker Slavoj Zizek in his latest book (*Violence*, 2008), such examples of bluff flim-flam are becoming increasingly common around the world, as politicians try to increase popularity for a profession now drained of any serious ideological content—their only genuine post-Cold-War role, according to Zizek, being that of mere caretakers—by trumping up spurious threats that create a simulacrum of drama and passion. For this to work, all they have to do is take local prejudices into account. If for Palin, for instance, it's abortionists that do the trick and for Chávez, yankee spies, then for for Russia's Putin, it's NATO and the Chechens; for Italy's Berlusconi, it's Italian Gypsies; and for Spain's Mariano Rajoy (and countless other Castilian politicos on both "right" and "left") it's (usually) the Catalans. And when it isn't, as any long-term resident knows, it's (usually) the Basques. Round and round, year after predictable year, ad nauseam. Until, of course, the fat lady finally sings, and I don't mean Montserrat Caballé.

Life Without

On my father and I

Catalonia Today, 24 October 2008

Banda Sonora [Soundtrack] is a weekly programme on Barcelona TV in which guest interviewees talk about their lives while listening to snippets of their favourite music. The director, Josep Morrell, and his team do a thorough job, with a lengthy pre-interview, discreet filming of the subject going about his or her daily routine, followed by a spotlit studio interrogation.

Last week, the interviewee, reader, was me. As usual on the few occasions when I have to watch my fat face on the small screen, I got tanked up before the broadcast but started to relax when I saw they hadn't manipulated the material for cheap effect (as is now the norm on TV everywhere).

I was, however, surprised to find that I'd talked so much to camera about the conflict between me and my father, which—although it lasted a good twenty years—I normally keep quiet about. Neutralish though my comments were, when they coincided onscreen with old photos of Dad, it made him look a bit like the villain of the piece. For many years, indeed, I had treated him as such; I blamed him for everything seriously wrong with me, until I finally grasped that our evergreen contention could not be pinned on him and him alone, we being equal victims of that well-known institution the family, which has a nasty tendency to make kith and kin of completely incompatible people.

Had I come to this conclusion earlier, I would surely have assured him to his face, on more than one occasion, just how much I loved him. Instead of waiting until the last time I saw him, when I whispered that secret into his ear as he lay eyes shut, in a London hospital, three weeks before his end.

Forked Tongue

On a cocked up Welsh road sign and similar blunders

Catalonia Today, 7 November 2008

I'd hardly been back in the UK a day when I heard about the recent Swansea Signpost Cock-up. Given that bilingualism is mandatory for official signs in Wales, when the functionaries of this Welsh city found they needed to put up a new road sign, they sent off their English original to a translator, unaware that he wasn't available. They got a reply nonetheless and duly transcribed it, with the result that the said sign warns drivers in English that there is "No entry for heavy goods vehicles. Residential site only," while telling the same drivers in Welsh: "I am not in the office at the moment. Please send any work to be translated."

The editor of a Welsh-language magazine pointed out that mistranslations of this kind are as commonplace as they are unnecessary (teeming as the country is with competent Welsh speakers). If such mistakes are made, he hinted, it was because the people responsible don't really care, Welsh being for them a complementary, minor-league vernacular to which only the most token of lip services need be paid.

Much the same attitude, indeed, was shown in Spain a few years ago by the Ministerio de Sanidad y Consumo, whose Basque-language version of an anti-drug poster campaign had the ministry urging the youth of Euskadi to consume all the dope they could handle.

In Catalonia, at least, such blunders are rare, for the simple reason that nearly all the signs posted directly by the Spanish government are monolingual. According to its plaque, for example, the *Delegación del Gobierno en la Comunidad Autónoma de Cataluña* is that and nothing more. A pity, because it'd be cute if directly underneath it read: *Ara mateix no hi sóc, a l'oficina. Si us plau, envieu-me els textos que voleu que tradueixi.*

Cupboard Love

On giving a talk in London
on anti-Catalan prejudice

Catalonia Today, 20 November 2008

Last Guy Fawke's Night, before an audience of about 45 people, in a mildly stuffy room, booklined and whitewashed, belonging to the Spanish department of the London School of Economics, I read out a 50 minute lecture on *Anti-Catalan Prejudice in Spain Today*. It began with some recent true stories of Catalans being refused service, insulted, or threatened with violence when at large in non-Catalan Spain. It then gave as potted a version as possible of relevant Catalan history, including the forced incorporation into the fledgling Spanish state in 1714, the two 20th century fascist dictatorships and the current miring of the Statute of Autonomy. It listed some of the 150-odd decrees designed to eliminate the Catalan language over the last two centuries. It broke anti-Catalan prejudice down into its three major clichés: the Catalans are treacherous separatists, persecutors of Castilian, and money-grabbing I'm-all-right-Jacks. And finally, it charted the origins of such mis-preconceptions from the late 18th century—when they first appear—through to the present. (The *full text can be found* earlier in this book.)

The audience reaction ranged from surprise to critical curiosity, but never strayed beyond the bounds of the rational. Afterwards, however, I was buttonholed by a middle-aged to elderly Spaniard who had kept mum during the Q&A. "I LOVE Catalonia," he spluttered (in perfect English), cheeks a-tremble and eyes aflame, "I LOVE Catalan culture." He jabbed my chest. "But it must be SHARED with all Spain. The Catalans want to keep it for THEMSELVES!" Another jab. "YOU are an EXTREMIST, like some of THEM!" It was as if the very title of the lecture—*Anti-Catalan Prejudice in Spain Today*—had materialised before me, ectoplasm-like. Albeit in its most liberal, generous, open-minded form.

Finko, Finko, Finko

On how Franco turns out to have been even more repulsive than previously thought

Catalonia Today, 20 November 2008

I've finally got round to reading Paul Preston's definitive biography of Franco Francisco Bahamonde (which first came out in 1993). If I dithered for over a decade, it was because I preferred not to so much as glance at a word about a man who had managed to commit two parallel atrocities in the only corner of the Spanish state that feels to me like home. In Catalonia—just as he did all over what he called "occupied Spain"—he signed the death warrants of Republican prisoners in sheaf-loads. But here, he also eliminated an entire culture, exiling or murdering its protagonists, bonfiring their books, and putting millions of Catalan-using citizens under a thuggish linguistic curfew for a third of a century.

Preston, however, reveals that General Franco was far more ruthless than even his Catalan curriculum would indicate. In Spanish Morocco, his legionnaires went on parade with native heads impaled on their bayonets. It was a short step from there to treating "Reds" in similar fashion: during the Civil War his troops regularly murdered, raped, and mutilated the inhabitants of captured cities. In the early '40s, with fuel reserves that wouldn't have lasted a long weekend and whole swathes of Spain bereft of the most basic foodstuffs, he did his level best to plunge his country into the Second World War, on the fascist side. Most frustrating of all, though, is to read how time and again he failed to come a cropper at the hands of a host of enemies, from Spanish monarchists to international anarchists, none of whom quite succeeded in euthanising this muddle-headed mass-murderer. Had they done so, Spain and Catalonia would surely both be something other, and something better, than the shaky survivors of a worst-case scenario that they remain today.

Matthew Tree

The Day After

On Saint Stephen's Day

Catalonia Today, 8 December 2008

That Christmas Day is often fraught with intra-family tension is a secret so open it's practically a platitude. As I remember it from childhood, after every Christmas lunch me and my cousins would lie belly up in a bloated stupor on the outskirts of the dining table, while the grown-ups, still seated, went on inexplicably helping themselves to drink although there was no food left to make them thirsty. Our senses, blurred though they were by surfeit, managed to detect the mood brewing, if not the actual words being noisily voiced. Whenever one of these domestic discussions grew loud—and there wasn't a one but did—we young persons would crawl within kissing distance of the TV to watch James Bond murder his malformed enemies and get the girl. Eventually, the adults' kerfuffle would peter out like a faulty banger, and the day would end with my family's car's doors being slammed shut under a cobweb-grey sky and back home we'd drive and that would be Yuletide that.

The following day, called Boxing Day in the UK, from when the well-off would drop leftovers in the begging boxes of the hopeful poor, never failed to be a washout, marking as it did the first sign of droop in the until then universally sustained Xmas arousal. So what a pleasure it was to discover, decades later, that the Catalan version of Boxing Day—*el Dia de Sant Esteve*—is, on the contrary, celebrated to the hilt, with all the frills, just like a second Christmas. With the advantage that any tiffs on the 25th have passed into history, allowing us all to bask, glowing with genuine affection and healthily drunk, in the true Christmas spirit, kept on a firm hold, as it were, for 24 happier hours.

More Con Than Mist

On inaccuracy and prejudice
in *The Economist*

Catalonia Today, 3 January 2009

I'd hoped that by this time Economistgate would be old, even dog-worried hat, but no, this sad controversy is still with us. The story so far: in its November 8th issue, *The Economist*, a self-described "authoritative weekly newspaper" based in the UK, published a special report on Spain. Mixed in with some pertinent economic analysis was a blithe chunk of Catalan-bashing, in which the Catalan language was assumed to be a nationalist-imposed hindrance to the economy, and the Catalans themselves, or their elected representatives, little more than a selfish bunch of apple-cart upsetters who had foolishly brought down upon themselves the opprobrium of all sensible Spanish people.

The article caused a whale of a splash, being announced on the evening news, commented on for weeks on end in Catalan newspapers both great and small, and, above all, causing thousands of citizens, whether Catalan or foreign, to send emails of correction and complaint.

The Economist waited three whole weeks before allowing a word of any of this to appear on its letters page. By which time, it had apparently received two "balancing" opinions to contrast the two pro-Catalan ones (which latter, carefully documented, were from the Catalan Government's UK delegation and a Catalan professor at Princeton). One of the "balancing" letters was from one Helena Medina in New York who spun therein a tale of anti-Spanish persecution in Catalonia unhampered by a single shred of evidence. The second was signed by EB, who limited himself to a brief xenophobic barf: "Catalan politics is based on clumsy parochialism, dead-end linguistic nationalism, and an astonishing amount of whining...." *The Economist* should sign this gentleman up for their Madrid office on the double, as he obviously has just what it takes to be the Spanish correspondent for such an authoritative weekly: die-hard centralist prejudices combined with unadulterated ignorance of the porcine kind.

Matthew Tree

Guttersniped
On starting a book on racism
Catalonia Today, 30 January 2009

I've just started to lie down in a bed made by myself and it already feels uncomfortable as hell. I knew what I was letting myself in for, so I thought, when I told the publisher that the next non-fiction book would be about racism. After all, I'd been surrounded by it all my life, racism being, as it were, very much in the European air. Wayward racist thoughts had occasionally even slipped into one of my ears, shaming the brain before they came thankfully out of the other. I'd also read plenty about slavery and lynchings in the US and I was even more conversant with the Shoah, including all the years of beard-cutting and shop-boycotting that preceded the bullets in the nape and the shoves into pitch black chambers.

Nonetheless, I was surprised, having begun to lower myself into the collective mental sewer of my chosen subject, just how unplumbed its depths were. None deeper, than those which revealed how the perpetrators of the above-mentioned crimes felt fully justified thanks to a series of ideas put in place, albeit unwittingly, in some cases, by countless European thinkers and scientists, eminent figures all, such as Fichte, Carlyle, and Herder with their concept of national character deriving from "blood", which later (1853) helped the novelist Joseph Arthur, Count of Gobineau to "demonstrate" inequalities between different "races", before passing on his venom-smeared baton to Houston Stewart Chamberlain (1855-1927), the once reputable English philosopher (now considered mad as a March hare) who gave both NSDAP leaders and Mississippi yokels a theoretical green light to mix wilful stupidity with gratuitous violence and so put those ubiquitous smug smiles on the photos (which I have to look at every day now) of Aryans young and old as they jeer at dead mutilated niggers and soon-to-be-dead cowering Yids. If only it was all a thing of the past. If only!

Teen Spirit

On the teenage Picasso's life in Barcelona

Catalonia Today, 26 February 2009

By an offhand coincidence my copy of last month's *Catalonia Today,* with its cover story on Picasso (Andalusia, 1881–France, 1973) arrived on the very day I started to read my first book ever about this painter, written by an author quoted in the opening sentences of the lead article in question: Josep Palau i Fabre. His *Picasso i els seus amics catalans* (1970) describes the painter's life as a young hopeful in Barcelona.

Having always regarded Picasso as a century-straddling, almost timeless figure, it was an eye-opener to discover that when he was a teenager he spent much of his time hanging out in bars with a bunch of other young prospects, uncertainty weighing heavily on their aspirations to future greatness. Among his chums, most of them forgotten today, was Ramon Reventós, whose short stories Picasso would illustrate 50 years later. And Jaume Sabartés, who at 19 finally gave up writing poetry in order to become a full-time Picasso devotee. And Benet Soler, the tailor, with whom Picasso and the others exchanged sketches for smart suits. And Manolo Hugué, the thief turned sculptor, who fascinated Picasso with graphic accounts of Raval low life. And Carles Casagemas, the closest friend, whose shotgun suicide in 1901 triggered off the painter's Blue Period.

There were also some well-known members of the crème of the local cultural crème: Casas, Rusiñol, Junoy, Gargallo, Vallmitjana, and Picasso's favourite painter at the time, Isidre Nonell. In this forward-looking, turn-of-the-century Catalan world, Pablo Picasso—Pau to his friends—felt so completely at home, that for the rest of his life, most of it spent in exile, he proudly insisted on speaking Catalan to his many visitors and friends from the Principality. Feeling as he did—so his widow hinted in a 1980 interview—that his birthplace was one thing, but his true native country, quite another. And there was I thinking I couldn't possibly have anything in common with such a towering genius.

Matthew Tree

Pieces of Cake

On speaking at a political rally for the first time

Catalonia Today, 28 March 2009

At the tail end of February I spoke in public at a political rally for the first time ever, despite belonging to that majority of citizens who wouldn't trust a politician any further than they could throw him or her. At the event in question, which took place at the Auditori in Barcelona, I had to present Oriol Junqueras, Esquerra Republicana de Catalunya's independent nominee for the European elections. In my defence, I could allege that Oriol is as smart as they come, honest as the day is long and talks only of things he knows about, qualities which would make him virtually unique among Euro MPs. What really decided me, though, was his insistence that my presentation be purely personal and apolitical.

I duly steeled myself to face an audience I supposed to be similar to those I had addressed before—in libraries, secondary schools, bookshops and prisons—who expect to be galvanised into pricking up their ears by all the energy the speaker can muster. I hadn't realised that at a party rally, the crowd is already wide awake and 100% on your side. Even my two-word opening greeting, *bon vespre*, got clapped to bits.

Talking to a politically motivated audience was so like falling off a log, I finally understood why politicians, spurred on by such sectarian goodwill, never failed to push for the maximum amount of easy applause by the tried-and-tested, equally easy ploy of slagging off rival parties. Thus generating those endless strings of tit-for-tat sound bites quoted daily in the dailies. Which guarantee the absence of any important issues whatsoever in party politics. Thus encouraging more and more people to ignore the ballot box. Which is why political parties are increasingly using non-card-carrying outsiders—like Oriol Junqueras—to restore their near-dead credibility. And why, presumably, these same outsiders prefer to be presented by other outsiders who (as in my case) are so credibly beyond the pale, they can't even vote.

Zora! Zora! Zora!

On Zora Neale Hurston, a writer lionised
and then unceremoniously ditched

Catalonia Today, 1 May 2009

The once lionised African-American writer Zora Neale Hurston started to make herself unpopular in the wake of Pearl Harbour, when she claimed the Japanese were no better or worse imperialists than the US themselves. This was the first of a cavalcade of discombobulating opinions that would result in their voicer being ostracised by those—both black and white on both left and right—whose own were more received than personally conceived.

All this and a lot more is explained in her autobiography, *Dust Tracks On A Road*, which I discovered just a handful of days ago. Her ductile style hits the spot time and time again. Even her takes on tiny details stick in the crop, as when she describes her white mistress's ludicrous lapdog: "...with his short legs, when he thought that he was running, he was just jumping up and down in the same place", as does her now famous comment on her mother's recommendation to her children that they try to "jump at de sun": "We might not land on the sun, but at least we would get off the ground."

But when, in the same book, she came out with statements like: "It [black race consciousness] is a deadly explosive on the tongues of men. I choose to forget it", such freethinking would soon consign her to the remorseless oblivion reserved for politically unfashionable authors.

By the time she died in 1960, her books were already as hard to find as her unmarked grave would turn out to be when posthumous admirers went hunting for it in the mid-1970s. Perhaps the most idiotic question that an interviewer ever asked me about a book of mine was "Do you think people'll be reading it in 50 years?" Please, I don't give a shit. Just spare me the fate of Zora Neale Hurston and so many other writers who managed to jump way off the ground, only to be buried alive under the self-serving orthodoxies of their respective times.

Matthew Tree

The Long Hello
On the correspondence between
Mercè Rodoreda and Joan Sales
Catalonia Today, 31 May 2009

The tail end of 2008 saw the publication of a thousand page correspondence between the writer and publisher Joan Sales and the novelist Mercè Rodoreda. Joan Sales is the author of *Incerta Glòria*, an epic modern classic (which, when it appeared in French just two years ago, was hailed by *Le Monde* as the finest Civil War novel to have come out of Spain).

Sales returned to Barcelona from his post-war Mexican exile in 1955 and founded Club Editor, which his perseverance would eventually turn into a major Catalan-language publishing house. Not least because its star author was, precisely, Mercè Rodoreda, whose fiction would end up translated into 33 languages, from Croatian to Chinese. All this despite the fact that when they started off, in 1960, most of the Principality's population had lost the habit of reading Catalan, thanks to Franco's post-war ban on books in that language, added to which the mostly regime-friendly media in Barcelona silenced each and every title which slightly slacker censorship laws then allowed to appear in Catalan.

When Rodoreda, exiled in Geneva, wrote to say she didn't understand why her masterpiece *La plaça del Diamant* was selling so slowly, Sales, by way of illustration, explained that books sales were plummeting in New York, due to a recent two month newspaper strike there (and so an inevitable dearth of reviews). "You have to understand," he went on, "that Catalan literature has had to live with its own 'newspaper strike' since 1939."

So it must have been quite impossible for either Sales or Rodoreda to imagine that 49 years later—on the 7th of May last—the tears would roll out of the eyes of a famous Hollywood actress (Jessica Lange) as, moved beyond self-control, she recited extracts from the English version of *La plaça del Diamant* before a mesmerised audience. In New York, once home of that illustrative two month newspaper strike.

On Draft

On common quasi-racial
anti-Catalan prejudices

Catalonia Today, 6 July 2009

Whenever the African-American jazz drummer Art Blakey sensed any (racial) prejudice heading his way, he would say he could "feel a draft". It'd be silly to equate the bigotry experienced by black people in white-majority nations with what happens to Catalans here, but surely an old friend, Jaume, must have felt some kind of a draft when a fellow guest he was chatting with at a wedding in Madrid told him, without a speck of irony, "For a Catalan, you're a really friendly guy!"

Not being Catalan myself, I have only felt such drafts vicariously: as when the English owner of a (failing) Barcelona production company assured me TV3 boycotted everyone who didn't have a Catalan surname (this was in the '80s, when, among other foreign employees, an Italian was the head of graphic design at TV3); or the Argentinian woman who was convinced that Catalan bosses were (without exception) far worse than Spanish ones.

Such minor gusts are as nothing, of course, when compared to the hateful gales of yesteryear, when centralists such as the Castilian novelist Pío Baroja or the Francoist apologist Antonio Luis de Vega vented their chronic anti-semitism—there being no real Jews to hand—on the Catalans, whom they regarded as "markedly Semitic" (Baroja, 1907) and "agents of a Zionist plot to rule the world" (de Vega, 1938). Milder though the winds of intolerance now are, one loathed Catalan stereotype still gets the goat of certain expats: that legendary bloodyminded Catalan who insists on speaking his local lingo even to people who don't understand it.

Recently, there has been an updated take on this nameless phenomenon: a mysteriously unlocatable Catalan police station in which people are refused help unless they speak Catalan. So, apparently, that earlier bloodyminded Catalan has now joined the Mossos d'Esquadra. If you run into this linguistic miscreant, do let me know. I'd love to meet him in the flesh, after all these years.

Matthew Tree

Beached

On the horror of beaches

Catalonia Today, 8 August 2009

"Hell is other people," wrote Sartre in his 1944 play, *No Exit*, although he could have been a lot more precise than that, if he'd ever found himself stuck by some stroke of unluck on a RENFE train going from Barcelona to anywhere on the Catalan coast—crammed tighter than a pig truck with vacant-eyed trippers clutching bags full of towelling and chemicals, their flimsy clothes covered in colours clashing so hard they could be collared for disturbing the peace—on a Saturday morning in the summertime, with a hangover. Never, once the train had crawled to a halt at Caldetes or Altafulla, say, had he been shaken out like so much cereal from its box, alighting in blinding light before shuffling his way onto crammed sand on which he would then have sat or stretched out with the rest of us, playing Russian roulette with ultraviolet carcinogens and gawping at an unreachable horizon, while the wind blew his newspaper into a paper irritation and the surrounding sound (kids' screams, family gabble, incompatible musical snatches) made it impossible, anyway, to read anything more difficult than the slogans on his neighbours' tattoos. Hell? Sartre didn't know the half of it.

As a teenager I used to cherish the idea of basking on a Mediterranean beach, palm trees in the background, beautiful girls (sic) a dime a dozen all around me, tepid water lapping sand so fine you could tell the time with it. So when I finally made it to Catalonia ten years later, I made it all but mandatory to spend every warm weekend by the seaside, fancying myself as happy-go-lucky as those beautiful, though apparently lobotomised, young things who used to swan about in the 1980s Martini ads. Middle-aged now, I much prefer the mountains. There, I get to keep my T-shirt on. Thus hiding the flab. Which helps curb my mortification should any beautiful girl (sic) happen to cross my path.

Hootenanny Reunion
On a nostalgic wallow in a large London pub
Catalonia Today, 31 August 2009

Before someone had the idea of naming it *The Hootenanny* after the American word for an improvised folk-music singalong, the pub on the corner of Effra Parade and Brixton Water Lane (London) was called the George Canning. Last August, I went back there for the first time in two decades. It was still as big as two barns and hadn't lost its stage or its long darkwood bar. I arrived ahead of time but it wasn't long before Max—organiser of our get-together—stepped in with Mal and Winston and there we were: four middle-aged men indulging in a little hard-earned nostalgia for the early 1980s, when we were thinner, bereft of grey hair, and at a permanent loose end, in part courtesy of the politics of a hawk-with-a-perm who had often declared publicly in a piercing voice that unemployment in Britain would remain high for at least ten years.

Trapped though we were, then, in the amber of the dole, it is those Brixton years—the heart of which was ever to be found in the Canning—that I still most miss: Mal and his collection of knives the shark one of which he pulled on a man who was persistently bothering his girlfriend one evening, making the eyes pop out of our table neighbours; the elderly cross-dressing busboy who used to waltz in his tutu from table to table at closing time screeching "fuck off the lot of you"; all of us sitting glued to the video juke-box to watch Jackson light up the pavement in "Billie Jean", the odour of discreet weed and lager-stained wood, music to our nostrils; and all Brixton milling around, from the funereal-faced dope dealers to the eco-artists in Peruvian sweaters, from the dedicated lesbian cadres to the soused old locals, from the ex-boxer behind the bar to Winston and Mal and Max and me, the alcohol sizzling behind our eyes as we laughed, and laughed, and laughed, swinging on our loose end, squirming in our amber.

Matthew Tree

Passport to Arenys

On the immense ruckus caused by the Arenys de
Munt poll concerning Catalan independence

Catalonia Today, 2 October 2009

Passport to Pimlico was one of sixteen Ealing Comedy films made in England between the late 40s and the late 50s, their plots characterised by the occurrence of outlandish events in markedly uneventful places. In recent weeks the inhabitants of Arenys de Munt, a village near Mataró, have found themselves plunged into a situation the Ealing scriptwriters would have rejected as way too implausible: the Village Council decided to hold a ballot to determine if the local citizens wanted Catalonia to become an independent state or not. It was then threatened with a potentially violent protest by the Falange de las JONS, a (Spanish) ultra-nationalist organisation which had flourished under Franco before withering into a weed of its former self under democracy. The Spanish government not only authorised this far-right demonstration, but ordered an (ex-Falangist) judge to ban the little village ballot.

This generated so much media attention that on the day the ballot was held (September 13th), Arenys de Munt had become a household name to millions and was duly flooded by thousands of independentist well-wishers and three hundred journalists and less than a hundred Falangists who gave the fascist salute protected by four hundred Catalan policemen while two thousand six hundred and seventy-one villagers voted a resounding ninety-six per cent "Yes" to an independent Catalonia, a result reported the day after by the *New York Times*, *Le Monde*, *Zeit*, *De Telegraaf* and *Reuters*. The day after, a whole flock of Spanish and pro-Spain Catalan politicians, their feathers ruffled into dishevelment, clucked jumpily about how the Catalans had to embrace only moderate political options.

Presumably in order to demonstrate the desirability of such options, a think-tank affiliated to Spain's conservative party formally recommended armed intervention in Catalonia, with all that would inevitably entail: tanks in the streets, mass arrests, sealed borders... All because of a village opinion poll! As a visiting English friend put it recently, "Spain's a fallacy, in the end." And the end, think many, is nigher than it ever was.

No Flowers

Written in haste on the eve
of a first trip to America

Catalonia Today, 11 November 2009

I write this just two days before visiting the United States of America, on a freebie but not a junket: I have to sing for my ticket in the form of a lecture, a round table and a live reading, together with Najat El Hachmi, Patrícia Gabancho, Sam Abrams and Simona Skrabec, that is to say, a scattering of us Catalan language writers who, having been born on foreign soil, can be wheeled out on occasion to surprise audiences abroad; but what makes this particular cat (please forgive the involuntary beatnik-speak) feel he's got the cream is that we are being to sent to San Francisco; San Francisco, where the City Lights bookshop—whose founder Lawrence Ferlinghetti published the banned poem "Howl" that author Allen Ginsberg yelled out for the first time in the city's Six Gallery in 1955—still flourishes; and just east of San Francisco is Oakland, where the Black Panthers were founded in 1966: the only armed liberation movement in the Western World that got widespread support from the population it was claiming to help; and just south of Oakland is Stanford University, Palo Alto, home to psychologist Philip Zimbardo's 1971 prison experiment in which he demonstrated, by randomly dressing up some students as guards as some as prisoners, just how dangerous people become when put in a uniform: any people, in any uniform; and just south of Palo Alto is Big Sur, home to the museum dedicated to Henry Miller, my favourite writer, invisible mentor and only hero, who lived on that coastal bluff—now a State Park—for 17 years and who wrote exactly as he pleased, having booted all and any mental censors out of his brain; as had Allen Ginsberg, and as had most of Ginsberg's fellow Beat Generation writers who gadded about in 1950s California, including Jack Kerouac who was leery of full stops and wrote without rewriting, following Ginsberg's maxim of "First is best" which is how, just for once, time being scarce, this article has been written or has written itself.

Matthew Tree

Quim Monzó: A Profile

On the Catalan writer Quim Monzó

Catalonia Today, 11 January 2010

At 57, he is The Writer in capital letters, an author considered so important that he now has an entire exhibition dedicated to his life and work that will run until April of 2010 (at the Arts Santa Mònica, at the foot of Barcelona's Rambla). His prolific output and high sales (some of his titles have sold a quarter of a million copies in Catalan alone) are not enough in themselves to explain such reverence, and here he is revered, dislike it though he does.

What made and makes him truly special is that starting with his first novel, published back in 1976, he has single-handedly post-modernised Catalan writing with his even blend of popular culture, pornography, fantastic realism, high comedy, stream-of-consciousness narrative, parody, absurd names for characters, and a thorough unpredictability of plot. Cohering it all is Monzó's personal take on a world he sees as both cruelly bleak and irresistibly funny. As good an example as any of what this means in practice is his only novel available in English—*The Enormity of the Tragedy*—in which a man wakes up with a permanent erection and attempts to copulate it away before discovering it's the symptom of a rare illness which will kill him in a matter of weeks. Less fuss, perhaps, has been made about Monzó's newspaper articles, all available in nine separate anthologies. It is here—in a format that in lesser columnists' hands tends to lend itself to glibness, false transgression, or the easy use of cliché—that Monzó's aversion to the hackneyed and the trite has resulted in hundreds of short pieces which land their blows as powerfully as does his best fiction. The culmination of his non-fiction work was surely his opening speech at the Frankfurt Book Fair in 2007 (Catalan culture was the fair's special guest). He read out a hybrid of article, short story, and nonsense verse that caused an instant stir of admiration among his international audience. Indeed he has been an international writer almost from the get-go, as James Ellroy (or any other American) would put it. Monzó's work has been successfully translated into 19 languages, including Dutch, Hungarian, German, Italian, Spanish, Russian, and Romanian. A pity, though, that the one in which he is least present for the present, is English.

Najat El Hachmi: A Profile

On this Moroccan-born Catalan writer

Catalonia Today, 11 January 2010

Even Catalans who don't know her from Eve refer to her casually as "Najat", such a household name has she become since 2008, when she won the Premi Ramon Llull—the most prestigious and best-remunerated award available to Catalan-language fiction writers—for her novel *L'últim patriarca [The Last Patriarch]*. Since then the novel has been translated into eight languages (the English edition will be out in March) and has aroused considerable interest in Hispanic literature faculties around Europe and the United States.

The quality of this truly well-written novel—which ranges from the ironic and comic to the downright upsetting in its description of a Moroccan family's migration to a (never-named) Catalan provincial town—is the root cause of its success, but the fact that a work of such quality should have been written by a 28 year old woman who didn't move to Catalonia herself until she was eight years old, has proven to be a positive surprise factor.

Najat's triumph came as less of a surprise to those of us who had read her first book, *Jo també sóc catalana*, a largely autobiographical work that had appeared four years earlier, providing proof enough that she was the real McCoy, a vocational author who would keep on keeping on. When *L'últim patriarca* made its first big splash, El Hachmi was instantly pigeonholed as an exemplary "integrated immigrant writer", a label she rejects as vehemently as if it were an accusation, maintaining as she does that she is an example of nothing or nobody except herself. Brought up a Muslim but one no longer, she will nonetheless have no truck with the endless media-prompted controversies over Catalonia's large Moroccan-born community, which more often than not are based on a biased and ill-informed take on Berber culture.

Those who get the chance to hear her speak about both her writing and writing in general—she gives quite a few talks a year in Catalonia alone—could do a lot worse than take it: they will find a humorous, coherent and thoroughly original author who won't take bullshit for an answer.

Matthew Tree

Before and After

On the English tendency to promote only English-language books

Catalonia Today, 7 February 2010

At the start of this year the London Guardian published a double feature called *Looking Back, Looking Forward*, about "the great writers" who had cashed in their chips over the last decade and those, still breathing, who were expected to excel in 2010. Of the 25 deceased since the year 2000, exactly two did not write in the language of Jamie Oliver (Naguib Mahfuz and WG Sebald). Of the 80 future titles singled out as "the best" of this new year, just three have been written in funny foreign lingos (Turkish, French, and Spanish).

There would be nothing too untoward about such bias were it not for the use of the definite article ("The great writers", "The best..."), a syntax implying that of all the writers in the world who passed away in what the English media has so very cringe-makingly named "the noughties"—as well as of all the thousands of books due to be published in the year 2010—people need only pay attention to two writers and three volumes of exotic alien provenance. Such literary presumptuousness—the notion that if a book isn't in English it can never really be the bee's knees, give or take the odd non-native genius—has been around since I was knee-high to my grandfather. According to K. David Harrison, the American author of *When Languages Die* (2008), it is this kind of attitude that ensured the enforced spread of global languages (English, Spanish, French, and so forth) in the colonial era, for which we are still paying the price. A steep one, according to the late linguist Ken Hale, who famously said: "When you lose a language... it's like dropping a bomb on the Louvre".

In the last decade, the world's global languages have blitzed 548 Louvres—from Ainu in northern Japan to Bororo in the Amazon basin—with another 2,500 or so slated for extinction by the mid-century. All in the name of "modernisation", "communication" and other familiar post-colonial excuses. But, hey, who's worrying, as long as "the great writers" can still be read in the language you're reading this tiny little wail of complaint in?

Space Cowboys

On *Avatar*

Catalonia Today, 3 March 2010

I'd always wanted to see a 3D film (when half-way through childhood, I pored over ads for a feature called *The Bubble*, filmed in "Spacevision": a vision I was too young to be allowed to have). So I made sure to see *Avatar*, whose 3-D technology—which took some 15 years to develop—is supposed to be, pardon my English, the dog's bollocks. At first, to tell the truth, I was put off by the killer rhinos slavering straight into the audience and the jungle bugs buzzing inches from my face, but as the minutes flowed on it dawned on me I was watching one of the most remarkable spectacles ever seen on a screen: waterfall-gashed mountains floating in pink skies, blue humanoids sprinting along fat kilometre-high branches, multi-coloured pterodactyls perching like butterfly colonies on distant crags... And yet. At the service of all this dazzle, the director had put a script so simplistic and over-familiar it might have been written by a pre-teen Friend of the Earth who had just discovered the meaning of the word "plagiarise".

The story line: on Alpha Centauri in 2154, an American mining company, seeing that the only thing standing between it and the minerals it craves is a tribe of Yanomami-like aliens, decides to send in a spy to gather strategic information, which is then used to bomb the locals off their land. When he sees the havoc he has helped wreak, the spy, outraged, spies no more and becomes the natives' leader. With his help and that of the local deity—a kind of eco-God—the indigenous people kick the Americans' environment-unfriendly butts back to their blighted world.

No brains need racking to remember where we've seen such themes before: *Dances With Wolves*, *A Man Called Horse*, *The Emerald Forest*... Altogether, then, *Avatar* is a confusing film. On the one hand, there are those jaw-droppingly stunning images, and on the other, a shoddily cloned script stuffed to the gills with Gaia theory platitudes. It's like having your breath taken way and being preached to by a very tedious hippie at the same time. For three hours. While a hail of undeserved Oscars gathers depressingly in the clouds above.

Eyeless in Fraga
On a nasty case of anti-Catalan hatred
Catalonia Today, 12 April 2010

Fraga is the capital of the Franja de Ponent: a strip of territory running along Aragon's border with Catalonia, in which Catalan is spoken by a higher percentage of the local population (a total of some 50,000 people) than anywhere inside Catalonia itself. Among these Aragonese Catalan-speakers is Joaquín, a Fraga-born friend of mine, who, when I visited his home town in March, told me about a new problem at work. He has a fixed stand at the ecological fruit and vegetable market held in Saragossa, the capital of Aragon, every second Saturday. As he buys his apples from Lleida, they arrive in boxes marked *Fruita de Lleida* 'Fruit from Lleida [Catalonia]'. For months, customers had been berating him noisily for daring to serve this blatantly Catalan produce, until the fair's organisers asked him to do something about it. So he put his apples in boxes marked *Plátanos de Canarias* 'Bananas from the Canary Islands' and since then has had no complaints.

This taken-for-granted loathing of everything Catalan is, he says, getting worse, in Saragossa and elsewhere as some friends of the journalist Patrícia Gabancho found out last year when they went to the El Prado gallery in Madrid. While commenting on a painting (in Catalan), a passing Spanish art-lover loudly informed them they were "Catalan bastards". The radio presenter Sílvia Tarragona got a similar reception in Madrid from the pickets at Radiotelevisón Española when she turned up for work during their 24 hour strike on March 3rd: "you shitty Catalan!", screamed the workers. This quasi-racial hatred blowing ever more strongly in from monolingual Spain, could well be the real reason why so many Catalans are quickly and quietly organising their multiple referendums for independence. Before I left Fraga, Joaquín told me about a Catalan girl who recently started going out with an Aragonese friend of his. When she visited her boyfriend's village, an elderly man came up, stuck a finger representing a gun barrel to her head and said "Catalan: bang, bang!". Let's hope Catalans will be able to enjoy the protection afforded by an independent state before such violent sentiments are expressed in—how shall we put it?—more physical terms.

Andorra, Mon Amour

On Andorra

Catalonia Today, 10 May 2010

Last month I set foot on Andorran soil for the first time in three decades. I'd come to think of this country in the way the Catalan media have come to present it in recent years—as a tiny annex to Catalonia. However, no sooner do you cross the manned border post, than you are clearly in another realm. Portuguese restaurants cater on every second corner to the 20,000 construction workers from that nation. Although Catalan is the only official language (and mandatory on all shop signs) not a Catalan flag is to be seen (the ubiquitous Andorran flag smacks uncannily of the Spanish Republican one). Indeed, native Andorrans deny they are Catalans, despite being brought up with Catalan culture and being, in the main, unconditional Barça supporters. (Pooh-poohing the Catalan government's consellers, Andorran ministers prefer to hob-nob with their opposite numbers in Madrid.) To achieve Andorran nationality, you have to reside in this valley of a country for all of 20 years. The steel and black glass of private banks—most with branches in distant tax havens—peek out brazenly from the endless strings of department stores and fast food restaurants. A public radio and TV station similar in size to the Catalunya Ràdio installations in Barcelona (which reach seven million people) broadcasts exclusively to just 60,000 Andorrans, a third of whom speak Catalan—the same third which presumably maintains the four Andorran dailies as well as two private radio stations. There are two cultural centres and one small bookshop. There is no unemployment, no income tax, and no army. There are sixteen known juvenile delinquents, who the police follow around like bloodhounds. The economy depends on winter tourism (expert Chileans and Argentinians man the snow equipment); on border tariffs (almost everything is imported); and on the locally grown tobacco, Andorra's only native product together with Andorran veal (considered the best in Europe). All the non fast-food restaurants are small padded leather, family-run affairs serving exquisite local cuisine. There is an average of three cars and two cellphones per citizen. The suicide rate is one of the world's highest. I really liked the place.

Matthew Tree

Legislating the Obvious
On the non-difference
between Valencian and Catalan
Catalonia Today, 2 June 2010

The headlines in the Barcelona press announcing—on May 6th last—that the Valencian government had finally accepted that Valencian and Catalan are one and the same language, didn't go round the world or even past the Pyrenees. Yet they marked an end to what surely must have been one of the most superfluous linguistic controversies on the planet.

Background: in 1232, Jaume I, the Count-King of Barcelona and Aragon, began to conquer the territory due west of Lleida (owned by the Caliph of Baghdad). By 1238, Jaume had taken Valencia City and went on to seize Alacant. He populated this newly acquired region, known in English as *Valencia*—which, in its final form, stretched from just beyond the Catalan border town of Ulldecona all the way south to Elx—with mainly Catalan settlers. A minority came from Aragon, which is why a snippet of the Valencian area is traditionally Spanish-speaking.

Over the following centuries, Valencia became a key part of the Catalano-Aragonese empire, in which Catalan was the universal language of administration, law, and commerce. In the 18th century the cultural ties between Valencia and Catalonia were loosened following their forced incorporation into Castile's new hegemonic version of Spain (the one we still live in today).

In the 20th century, to weaken the demographic importance of Catalan, the dictator Franco decreed that it was a completely separate language from Valencian (despite there being less difference between the two than between, say, Liverpudlian and Mancunian). Since then, the post-fascist right-wing in Valencia, headed by the governing Partido Popular, has toed Franco's linguistic line.

As a result, for decades teachers from Catalonia and Majorca with degrees in Catalan have had to take a separate degree in "Valencian" if they wanted to teach south of Ulldecona. This, at a time when Catalan writers were selling like hot cakes in Valencia and vice-versa, and when Catalan TV's soap operas—beamed over the border—were followed by tens of thousands of Valencian viewers with no linguistic difficulties whatsoever. So, after spending court fees amounting to 16,500 per taxpayer in countless attempts to demonstrate that Valencian is not Catalan, the Valencian government has finally ratified the self-evident fact that it is. So now we know: the world is not flat, the Holocaust happened, fairies don't live at the bottom of anybody's garden, and "bon dia" means the same up in Figueres as it does in down in Xàtiva. Phew!

Summer of Hate
On "non-racist" racist politicians
in Holland and Catalonia
Catalonia Today, 19 August 2010

On the 10th of June last, the highly coiffed Dutch politician Geert Wilders—leader of the Partij voor de Vreiheid (PVV: the "Freedom Party")—doubled his votes in the national elections, and may well become a minister in a future coalition government. This wouldn't be a problem if Wilders hadn't spent the last few years advocating the banning of the Koran in Holland. Like many of his political ilk in Europe, he denies he is a racist and claims his beef with the North Africans is a purely religious matter.

A quick scratching of his surface reveals this to be disingenuous. To begin with, his op-ed pieces in the Dutch press reveal he hasn't heard of the Hadiths, the narrative spin-offs from the Koran, so essential to Muslim belief they would presumably have to be banned as well. In other words, he knows next to nothing about the religion he wants to eliminate. Moreover, Wilders avoids mention of the 2.6% of the Dutch population made up of Indonesians, many of them Muslims—whom the Dutch consider as Dutch as they are—and concentrates on the less popular 2% who come from Morocco. In short, he is playing the old racist card, but face down.

If we've gone on so long about Wilders, it's because he has an exact equivalent here in Catalonia: Josep Anglada, the founder of the *Plataforma x Catalunya* party. As with the PVV, "PxC" is a misnomer: Anglada cares as much about Catalonia as Wilders does about Freedom (for example, the PxC

Matthew Tree

is opposed to the ongoing local opinion polls on Catalan independence). Like Wilders, Anglada has made the Moroccan community his first whipping boy, also on supposedly religious grounds alone. Again like Wilders, his party is expanding fast, as I found out when I started touring Catalonia to promote my latest book, which happens to be an essay on racism. In town after town, I was told that Anglada would soon be campaigning there. Surveys show he stands a fair chance of getting into parliament in the next Catalan elections. Once there, having got stuck in to the Moroccans, he'll then doubtless turn on the Africans and any other "racial" group that gets his goat. Something tells me, though, that us EU expats—as white as Anglada thinks himself right—will be spared his slurs. Have a great summer!

Runaround

On the anger generated by being buggered about by an airline and a railroad company

Catalonia Today, 3 September 2010

Gatwick airport, Saturday 14 August 2010, 6.30pm: we have been kept on tenterhooks, we passengers on flight EZY 5137 to Barcelona, with an initial delay of twenty minutes having been jumped up at autistic intervals to forty-five, then seventy, then ninety. Finally, a gate number pops up on the information panels, surprising as an unsolicited kiss, and off we go along relays of corridors into a departure lounge so tiny, over half of us have to stand. For forty minutes more. 8pm: the Easyjet rep apologises for the flight having just been cancelled. He leads us back along those corridors to baggage reclaim where we heft our untravelled cases and return to the check-in area to change our flight.

There are none to Barcelona, so they suggest one to Valencia, due to depart on Sunday night, and offer to put me up in a hotel meanwhile. 10.45pm: me and the other, mainly Catalan passengers (who, by the way, have had considerable difficulties understanding the garbled, unamplified, and monolingual instructions from the Easyjet staff) check in at the Gatwick Holiday Inn as fast as we humanly can, given that the Easyjet dinner vouchers expire within 15 minutes. We eat. We go to bed. Sunday, 10am: we sit around in the gilded limbo of the lobby, from which I book a seat on Monday morning's Valencia-Barcelona Talgo express.

4pm: I return to Gatwick airport and check in for the second time. 8pm: after a one and a half hour delay, I enter an aeroplane, and it takes me to Valencia. Monday, 1am: I check into Valencia's airport hotel. I sleep, badly. 9am: I take a taxi to Valencia's Estació del Nord. The RENFE's PA system informs me that my Talgo will be three hours late. It has been substituted by a ropey-looking bus, now standing ready on the station plaza.

No lover of long coach journeys, I look forward, at least, to catching up on some sleep. 10.30am: I am writing this article on that very bus because just as I was about to drop off, the drivers put on a boxing film at full blast. Russell Crowe—with whom I am identifying heart and soul—is loudly pummeling his rival (who I imagine to be Mr Easyjet and Mr Renfe combined) into pink mash. But, tell me, how might I get to these two travellers' nemeses in real life, so that they will really and truly get what's coming to them?

Smokescreen
On Catalonia's changed situation and its non-ethnic sense of identity
Catalonia Today, 9 October 2010

As soon as I got there—I mean here, Catalonia—at the end of the 1970s, I felt I'd stumbled on a local atmosphere whose openness and positive tension was not to be found in any other corner of Europe. 30 years on, evidence to the effect that this was not a late-teen hallucination has been accumulating. Even if we sideline, for reasons of space, specific recent strides made in Catalan-language culture—fiction, theatre, popular music—the non-ethnic Catalan concept of cultural identity in itself has proven to be unique, at least within the EU. How would the British, for instance, have reacted if in the last ten years over ten million people from the five continents had turned up on their island?

The proportional equivalent has happened here and despite the slight presence of a certain (pro-unionist) racist party and the intellectually-challenged electoralist blathering of some (pro-unionist) mainstream ones with regard to mosques and certain religious costumes, the most visible and popular Catalan reaction has been the exponential growth of the linguistic volunteer programmes, in which newcomers can learn Catalan—which in Catalonia means they partly *become* Catalan, as well as being what they already are—by meeting up with local people on equal terms and in normal places (not classrooms).

At the same time, all newcomers are being encouraged (also by volunteers, not politicos) to take an active part in what has become a generalised grass-roots debate over independence, as shown by the more than 200 towns and villages which have organised unofficial ballots for (or, if you vote thus, against) secession, the 50-odd municipalities which have declared themselves morally divorced from the Spanish Constitution, and a partly pro-independence, partly pro-federalist demonstration in Barcelona (on 10/7/10) involving one and a half million people.

The European media in general, and the English ones in particular, have excelled themselves in turning blind eyes to all this, mainly because, like Manuel in *Fawlty Towers*, they know nothing. As the historian Eric Hobsbawm pointed out years ago in his book *The Age of Extremes* (1994), not a single major historical event of late 20th century Europe—not even the implosion of the Soviet Union—was anticipated by the journalists. Soon, I suspect, the hacks are about to be caught out yet again. Watch this corner.

Year's End

On Jordi Cussà

Catalonia Today, 14 December 2010

Jordi Cussà, of whom I am both a friend and eager reader, is a live and prime example of an *écrivain maudit*: one of those writers consigned by Sod's Law to relative oblivion despite the undeniable quality of their work. Having survived the first part of his adult life—Cussà was involved in professional drug dealing, became heavily addicted to heroin himself and had five car crashes—he synthesised some of his experiences into a stunning novel called *Cavalls salvatges [Wild Horses]* which appeared in 2000 to critical applause.

It garnered him his first hardcore readers, who for the last ten years have been following his writing wherever it takes them: to the ancient world (*La serp*, 2001), to the jungles of South America (*L'alfil sacrificat*, 2003), to Sitges (*Apocalipsis de butxaca*, 2004), to an ultra-sophisticated realm of science-fiction (*La novel·la de les ànimes*, 2005), to a hilarious, delirious gospel tour (*Clara i les ombres*, 2007), on an emotive meander through a variety of short stories (*Contes d'onada i tornada*, 2009), to the Bosnian war (*El noi de Sarajevo*, 2010) and finally, at the tail end of this year, to a future Catalonia made independent both by hook and by crook (*A reveure, Espanya*).

Cussà has a rhythmic, flowing style which meshes high, low, and middle registers into a single natural voice exuding a conviction hard to find in most writers, let alone just Catalan language ones. When he occasionally grouses about his lot, you can hardly blame him. He has been shunted from publisher to publisher like a redundant tank engine, and his last four books have been largely ignored by the reviewers. However, a glimmer of hope has appeared on the new decade's horizon. His Bosnian novel will be published in Italian early in 2011.

With luck, it'll be followed up by more recognition and thus more translations (this article has been written in English, in the hope that some publisher, somewhere, will take the hint). Romantic though it might be to be *maudit*, there are few writers who don't look forward to the day when their particular curse will be finally lifted. It's more than high time that Sod let Jordi off the hook. Oh, and Happy Christmas.

Matthew Tree

Harvest Time
On death

Catalonia Today, 31 January 2011

Two people close to me lost one each of their parents over the recent Season of Good Cheer. This was not the first time death has pounded his beat in my immediate vicinity, but it has been a while. The last time he got close—closer, even—was back in 1994, when I was 35, and my father passed away (unless we count the time in 2007 when a doctor assured me, wrongly, that I had lung cancer, but that was hardly death's fault). Before 1994, death took my last grandparent away when I was in my mid-twenties and not long after, a dose of undiluted heroin put an end to the short life of a good friend.

But when young, it would seem, you can shrug death off almost as soon as the grieving ceases. Later in life, it gets harder to take that scythe on the chin any more. By then, you are far enough over the hill to have a clear view of what lies on the other side, and even though the downward slope is still green and fairly pretty-looking, the hooded figure killing time at the very bottom simply cannot be ignored.

Last week, one of the two people who had lost a parent at Christmas, my oldest friend Max, and I, discovered we'd both just begun to take stock of our lives: to look back. As it turned out, the only regrets we had concerned our non-private lives: Max hadn't yet scripted a full-length film and I hadn't yet published a full-length novel in English: two ambitions mutually confessed some three decades ago. I told Max I'd often imagined that at the end of a natural life people maybe feel something akin to the melancholy children often experience at the close of a longish summer holiday: endless though it had seemed at the start, suddenly they realise they won't be able to do all the many, many things they thought they had so much time to squeeze in. Having said which, Max and I determined to go on determinedly chasing our particular ambitions, come what may. Right up to the last gleamings, as it were, of our respective summers.

And to hell with the harvest.

Articles

This miscellaneous collection of longer pieces about different aspects of life in Barcelona and Catalonia includes material published in the *El País* newspaper, *The Journal of Iberian Studies*, and *The Times Literary Supplement*, among other publications.

Stranger in a Strange Land
20 Years of Living and Writing in Catalonia

This article, recently rediscovered (by me), originally published in the International Journal of Iberian Studies, *and subtitled "20 Years of Living and Writing in Catalonia", was read at an international symposium at Lancaster University in early 2005. It is a subjective account of the various problems involved in moving to a nationally ambiguous area such as Catalonia; and a discussion of the function of autobiographical writing for authors living abroad.*

Recent, even relatively recent, books by foreign writers on the part of Spain which I have lived in for the last twenty years—Catalonia, and, for that matter, the Catalan-speaking areas in general—are few and far between. What is more, the vast majority of these books are written by authors whose stance wishes to be formally objective, and who therefore present themselves as reporters, journalists, chroniclers, historians, and so forth. This is the case even in a book as impassioned as E. Allison Peer's *Catalonia Infelix*, published in 1937, in which this expert on Ramon Llull attempts to elicit his readers' sympathy for the plight of the war-torn Catalans. By absenting his own personal motives for writing, however, Peer tries to give the impression that his book is an objective account of a given situation, whereas any reader can see that the author feels strongly, feels desperate indeed, about his subject matter. But as we are not told why, the book ends up having a pamphlety feel to it.

Two other writers working in the same period, George Orwell and John Langdon-Davies, give magnificent accounts of their time in Catalonia. Both authors, however, are well-aware that they are writing—naturally enough—for a British readership, and this, consciously or unconsciously, conditions many of their observations, right down to homely touches that verge on journalistic travel-writing for the folks back home, such as Orwell's definition of chorizo, in *Homage to Catalonia*, as "that red sausage which gives you diarrhoea". Forty years later, authors like Jan Read and, more importantly, Colm Toibin, decided to write about the area, in two books, *The Catalans* and *Homage to Barcelona*, respectively, which provide invaluable introductions to readers unfamiliar with Catalonia. When it comes to making any kind of subjective value judgement, however, both authors prefer, in the last instance, to maintain what amounts to a detached, almost anthropological approach to the more controversial aspects of daily life in a notoriously complex area. (A curious exception to the general rule is the Canadian cookery writer Colman Andrews, whose *Catalan Cuisine* contains several convinced personal statements of a political and cultural nature, as well as a plethora of tasty recipes.)

The 1980s and 1990s saw the appearance of a new phenomenon: foreign authors writing about Catalonia in Catalan: the German Til Stegmann and the Japanese Ko Tazawa both produced books about how they saw Catalonia from their different national standpoints which became instant best-sellers within Catalonia itself. Once again, however, the personal element was largely missing. Stegmann limited himself to making a series of linguistic recommendations—somewhat pedantic ones, if we have to be honest—to the Catalans, and Tazawa concentrated on providing an objective description of how Catalonia was perceived in his own country.

Now, I know for a fact that this brief list of authors writing on Catalonia is incomplete—no mention has been made, for example, of Daniele Conversi's excellent 1997 report *The Basques, The Catalans and Spain*—but the point that is trying to be made here is that nearly all the writers mentioned have chosen, for one reason or another, not to deal with some of the deeper implications of writing about a foreign land. Certain key questions have remained unanswered. For example, what elements in their own personal lives have conditioned their views of this land? How do they view their own sense of nationality or of national belonging, and indeed, how do they evaluate the concept of nationhood itself? (A particularly pertinent question in the case of a nationally ambiguous area like Catalonia.) To what extent are they linked to this land? Do they have friends from there? Lovers and spouses, even? How long have they spent here and how has their stay affected their viewpoint? In which circles did they or do they move, what opinions did they or do they come across? (The sojourn of Allen Ginsberg and Gregory Corso in Paris in the 1950s springs to mind. For years they mixed almost exclusively with fellow Americans, a social set-up which must have conditioned their overall view of France.) Again, such questions are of even more vital importance in Catalonia, where the group of friends you fall in with will determine not only the kind of opinions you hear but also the very language you learn to speak.

I say all this because my own twenty-five year long relationship with Catalonia has been nothing if not subjective, and I am only capable of explaining it in purely subjective terms. When I was young and hysterical, my opinions about Catalonia were young and hysterical. When I reached an almost complete dead end in London, in my mid-twenties, it was to Catalonia that I turned when seeking a way out. In my thirties, when I'd been writing for so long that I finally managed to achieve a lifelong ambition and write something publishable, I wrote it in Catalan and it was Catalans who published me and Catalans who read me. And now, in my mid-forties, plagued by self-doubt and completely unsure of the future, it is Catalonia that provides the background, the beautiful background, against which all this middle-aged angst is currently being played out. There is something else, too. Never one for birthdays, I am nonetheless finding it increasingly hard to ignore the fact that this September will mark the twentieth anniversary of my arrival in Barcelona as a permanent resident. Twenty has a nice, round feel to it, and I daresay it is because of all this unavoidable roundness looming up on the horizon that over the last year and a half I have been given to increasingly long periods of reflection about the process of contact with and arrival in Catalonia, and all the years that have passed since then. The late Arthur Terry, at the end of his book on Catalan literature, famously quoted W.B. Yeats as saying that one's nation "is the only thing one knows even a little of". On the contrary, it seems to me that nations are mysterious organisms that defy any attempts to even define, let alone know, them, and that the only thing one really knows even a little of, when it comes down to it, is one's own subjective, personal experience. I hope you will therefore forgive me, if I use my personal experience as the principal material upon which I will base the comments that follow: that is to say, the rest of this paper.

Those of us who have lived for a long time in Catalonia are usually asked, sooner or later, about how integrated we feel. Many Catalans—for whom the whole concept of identity plays an important role in their lives—often come out with a sentence like: "After all this time, you're a Catalan like the rest of us." I, for one, tend to refuse this generous offer, simply because

I feel that, in the end, I am English by definition (not that I feel at home in England, but that's another story), given that that is where I was born and lived until twenty-six years of age, which is old enough for anyone to feel attached for life to a given place or culture. When pressed on the question—and believe me, the Catalans are good pressers—I come out with what seems to me the only truthful solution, and answer that I feel like an adopted Catalan, that Catalonia (not Spain, by the way, but that too is another story) is my adopted country.

This mutual adoption, however, and this is the case of many foreigners currently living in Catalonia, did not happen overnight. To begin with, there is a specific hurdle which needs to be overcome by those of us whose sense of national identity is so much taken for granted that it is virtually unconscious. To give an idea of why this hurdle exists precisely in Catalonia, we could do worse than describe what can only be called the identity surveys that are carried out in the area by both Spanish and Catalan government organisations, every two or three years or so. In these surveys, Catalans—that is, people *born* in Catalonia—are asked a bewildering range of questions about their sense of national belonging. They can choose, for example, between feeling only Catalan, more Catalan than Spanish, as much Catalan as Spanish, more Spanish than Catalan, and only Spanish. All categories have their adherents, although most belong to the first three, at least at the last count. I explain all this, so as to give some idea of what the newcomer faces when arriving in Catalonia for the first time. The great majority, though I suspect it is a shrinking majority, of European citizens still have no sense of ambiguity whatsoever when it comes to their own national and cultural identity. They are where they're from and that's it: their identity is a question of unquestioned common sense for them. Such citizens, upon arrival in a nationally ambiguous area such as Catalonia, have two options. They can either ignore the ambiguities altogether, and impose their own monocultural concept of common sense on the natives, considering them, in this case, to be Spanish and Spanish only (an option which only 3 per cent of the Catalans themselves believe in, according to the surveys), or they can try and come to terms with the ambiguities they find by gradually infiltrating Catalan society and eventually adopting a personal approach to it which allows them to feel comfortable in Catalonia without them having to close their eyes—not to mention their ears—to any aspect of what is, by any standards, a bafflingly intricate cultural and linguistic situation.

I have a vivid memory of my own mental struggles with the whole idea of Catalonia when I first arrived there. Convinced that Spain had a single national identity—like England, but not Britain of course—I could simply not visualise what you might call the role of Catalonia within Spain. When I went on a trip with some Catalan friends to monolingual central Spain my fretting reached an almost unbearable pitch. Where was I, exactly? What was the exact difference between Catalonia and the Spain I was now visiting? Could a country exist within another country, or was that just wishful thinking on the part of a sector of the Catalan population? If Catalonia was also Spain, why did some Spanish show a marked hostility towards Catalonia (and some Catalans towards Spain)? Later, I was relieved to find that I wasn't the only one who had wracked his brain in this manner. From the foundational text of Catalan nationalism—Valentí Almirall's *Lo catalanisme*, published in 1886—through to dozens of titles published every year since Franco's death, the Catalans have puzzled over, vilified, celebrated, defended, and criticised their peculiar condition as the heirs of a defunct 14th century empire and a defeated 18th century semi-state for nearly a hundred and twenty years.

This is neither the time nor the place to enter the maze of Catalanist—and, in part, anti-Catalanist—theory which the Catalans have built up over time. We would all get lost and besides, there is as yet no exit gate through which we could emerge into the wider world. However, a general observation is in order. To begin with, no matter how confusing I found Catalonia at first, I soon discovered one thing for sure: that the importance of language in the Catalan mindset cannot be overexaggerated. A citizen's relationship with Catalan—latent or visible—has effectively replaced the old 19th century concept of "blood" (universal throughout Europe then and, sadly, in many cases, even now) as a marker of identity. Catalans have little difficulty nowadays in accepting that someone from Cáceres or even from Karachi is a Catalan citizen, as long as this person's relationship with the language is a comfortable, albeit a passive, one, in other words, that the language is understood if not actually spoken. On the other hand, few would find it easy to describe as Catalan someone who couldn't understand at least basic Catalan (which is the case of a mere seven per cent of the population, by the way). This does not mean that Catalan-speakers are dogmatic about their use of language. Most switch from Catalan to Castilian and back again with practised ease on a daily basis, depending on who they are talking to. Some have even ended up all but eliminating Catalan from their social lives, without this implying rejection of the language, which is always present somewhere in the background, be it at home, or at work, or on TV and radio. There is also a relatively new phenomenon: some children of Castilian-speakers who prefer to use Catalan as their default language. And so on. I mention this so as to highlight the importance for the foreigner of the language question. Everyone is free to deal with this question as she or he sees fit, of course, but it is necessary to deal with it, to face up to it, to make a linguistic decision of some kind, and—languages being doorways into shared complicities as well as simple means of communication—that decision will condition the nature and degree of your integration into Catalonia. As I probably don't need to say by now, I learnt Catalan first. Castilian came along six years later and remains very much my third language. This has resulted in a sense of being correspondingly much closer to things Catalan than to things Spanish, with all that that entails in terms of books read, media consumed, sense of geographical attachment, linguistic behaviour, and so forth. I do not see my linguistic decision as being any better or worse than anyone else's. But I am pleased with it personally, it has resulted in me feeling entirely at home in my foreign land of choice for many years, and it has afforded me insights which a different decision would not have made possible. I do not wish to go beyond this statement of subjective satisfaction. I no longer like to suggest what people should or should not do when they arrive in Catalonia—as if I knew! After all, I made my decision on my own and that is perhaps the best way for anyone to make any decision, especially one as important as this.

*

And now for the hard part. Calliope Stephanides, the Greek-American hermaphrodite hero, or heroine, of Jeffrey Eugenides's Pulitzer prize-winning novel *Middlesex*, remarks at one point in the narrative that funerals have only one function, namely, to keep the bereaved so busy that they have no time to think about the deceased. Something similar could be said about people, at least Western European people, who make a conscious decision to change country. They become so wrapped up in the ins and outs of finding their feet in the host culture—learning a new language, perhaps, or looking for work, or trying to rebuild their social lives—that they conveniently forget about what is possibly the most important thing of all: themselves, the very people who are making the change. Who are they, at heart? What are their deeper motives for moving? What situations did they leave behind in their native countries? Besides, there is something giddying about changing country, something intoxicating, something that helps erase the past. You walk through foreign streets, past foreign people, smelling foreign food until it gradually dawns on you that you could be anyone, meet anyone, spin any old yarn about yourself to them, and be accepted by them on your own terms. In a foreign country, you can hobnob with people who would have been beyond the reach of your social spectrum back in the old country, you can rough it with the roughest at breakfast time and look high-flying multinational executives in the eye when taking your evening gin and tonic. There is no apparent limit to your mobility, because there is no need to explain yourself, no one will expect you to reel off your social curriculum—born here, studied this, worked at that—in an attempt to pigeonhole you, because they already have pigeonholed you, as a foreigner, that is to say, as British or French or whatever, and, at least at first, they require no more information from you. They might attach a few clichéd labels to you—if you're English you must be punctual, if you're French you have to be a gourmet, etcetera—but that aside, you are free to reinvent yourself at will. In the case of someone from Britain, where people still try to pinpoint someone's social class automatically upon meeting them by checking on their place of birth, current residence and, last but definitely not least, their accent, the social anonymity to be found when away in a foreign country leaves you with a feeling of instant relief that is absolutely breathtaking.

So it was that, once installed in Barcelona, I stowed my English past away in the deepest mental hold I could find. As a result, I not only became a much happier person but I found, once I had sufficiently mastered the host language, that I could write in it with much the same freedom and lack of awkward ballast that I was experiencing in my new social life. I wrote principally autobiographical stories and novels and books of non-fiction, which

Matthew Tree

dealt almost exclusively with personal events which had taken place in the host country. England—with the exception of a few burlesque episodes—barely got a look-in. I liked it like that. Accepted as simply one more of their writers, thanks to what I consider to be the Catalans' extraordinary capacity for integrating outsiders, I continued to publish over a period of some five or six years, happy as a sandboy, unaware that the monster in the hold had begun to stir.

You can stow the past away, but you can't throw it overboard, so sooner or later, it is going to make its presence felt, as it chafes about, frustrated with its cramped conditions. After nearly eighteen years of having lived abroad, I was finding the past—the pre-Catalan past, I mean—harder and harder to ignore. My early social freewheeling in Catalonia had slowly transformed itself into a more settled way of life. Yet the more outwardly settled I became, the more unsettled I felt deep down. This increasing discomfort was not helped by the fact that things, objectively, had gone fairly well, in the sense that I was basically living off what I'd always wanted to do—write—and so everyone expected me to be chirpy most of the time. So I felt the need to write a novel which would, I hoped, at least open the hatch of the hold, so to speak, and allow people the chance to peek in.

I wrote the novel. In general, the message didn't get through. Catalan readers who had been used to my earlier fictionalised accounts of life in Catalonia didn't understand or even like this new, much darker story set mainly in the UK. Stunned by this reaction, I ignored the good reviews and comments and rolled in the dung of the negative ones until I had convinced myself that as a writer, I stank: I was no good, I had reached the end of the line, I was a fraud, it was time to pull the plug. For about a year, I moped about on the verge of a self-induced despair, quite literally not knowing what to do with myself. Only then did it occur to me that there was just one way out: to go back to the autobiographical vein but this time in order to write as truthfully as possible about what had happened to me in the pre-Catalan years and what I felt about it. This confession, which poured out of me over a six month period, eventually became the first two thirds of the book recently published in Catalan with the title *Memòries!* Here, for the first time, I looked at the privileged English education—at both school and university—which I had not wanted and which I had always been deeply, obsessively ashamed of, and at the mental illness triggered, in part, by my inability to cope with the sense of guilt such an education had aroused in me. To give an idea of what writing this down for the general public meant to me, I need say no more than, before the publication of this book, my social background was known to just three of my closest friends—none of them in Catalonia—and my mental illness to them and perhaps half a dozen people more. Now, as it were, I was slapping the whole lot down on a canvas intended for open display. No wonder that, two weeks before the publication date, I almost chickened out and withdrew the manuscript. However, despite my quavering, the book came out, in March 2004.

I dreaded the reception it would get. I even mentally wrote some of the terrible reviews I felt sure it would receive and rehearsed the bad-mouthing I felt sure readers would give it. None of these things happened. Of the six titles I have published to date, none has produced anything like the kind of rewarding, personal, positive responses I have had for *Memòries!* What people identified with and reacted to was not so much the details of my life explained in the book, as the act of honesty implied by their telling. As a result they found points of contact, of self-identification, in the most unlikely episodes. To cut a long story short, after *Memòries!*, I no longer feel like a fraud. No matter what I do in the future, the truth, my truth, about the past, at least, is now there for everyone who wishes to, to see.

So it is, that I have come to the end of a long twenty year cycle in Catalonia, leading from fictional beginnings to an autobiographical conclusion. I would now dearly like to reconcile myself in a similar manner with the country in which I was born, which is the next challenge on the horizon.

To sum up, when we arrive in the foreign country we aspire to adopt, we can hide—and frolic happily—behind the mask that our status as outsiders provides us with. We can infiltrate the host society, if we so wish, with the deftness of master spies, putting on different guises for different social situations. But this masquerade can only go on for so long if we do not want to end up as cardboard characters. Sooner or later, we have to define ourselves clearly as individuals before the people among whom we live. We have to come clean. Autobiography, the writing of memoirs, is one way of coming in from the cold of the past, that is, of the time before we burnt our bridges and turned ourselves, willingly, into strangers in a strange land.

Matthew Tree

Letter from Barcelona

On four Catalans who are
in the writing business

21 June 2010

The patron saint known to the English as George is also that of another dozen or so countries, including Russia, Portugal, Georgia, Lithuania, Djibouti, and Catalonia (capital, Barcelona). Here, at least, the day assigned to this maiden-saving myth is celebrated without a smidgen of jingoism. Far from waving any national flags, for example, each Catalan citizen simply gives a book to at least one person he or she loves, be it husband, wife, daughter, son, boyfriend, girlfriend, auntie, or whatever; on top of which, the males (only) buy roses for all the women they know who might appreciate one. The 23rd of April, then, sees the centre of Barcelona chock a block with street stalls stacked high with volumes for which people reach and grab as if the printed word really was going out of fashion. On the metro and buses, even the staidest of besuited office workers can be seen gingerly bearing scarlet roses upright by their prickly stems.

This year on Sant Jordi's Day, Catalonia's 700-odd bookshops sold 20 million euros worth of titles in Catalan and Spanish (in roughly equal numbers), representing nearly 8% of total yearly sales. In that 12-hour period, Catalan language publishers grossed 34% of their annual turnover.

The following Monday, April 27th, Enric and Màrius and Bernat and Jordi—all of them involved in the writing business, one way or the other—sat down to their more or less regular monthly lunch, chatting even before they hit the chairs about the events and consequences of this latest book-and-rose day. By the time pudding was served, however, they had subject-hopped so swiftly that Sant Jordi was no more than a faint memory. When the coffees came, they finally bothered to ask each other what they themselves were getting up to. I sat back—being the fifth diner—impressed by the sheer abundance and quality of their output, both past and present.

Enric (Gomà) is one of the pioneers of the home-grown soap opera in the Peninsula, into which he introduced the form back in 1993 through his work for Catalan-language TV. Despite the language "barrier" his products were noticed and emulated throughout both Portugal and mono-lingual Spain. The long-running soap he is working on now for Catalan Public TV gets regular audiences of about a million per episode. He is also a well-known writer of children's books, contributes two satirical articles a week for a major newspaper and *Time Out Barcelona* respectively, and is the founder and internet coordinator of a bizarre collection of overheard snip-pets of street conversation, in half a dozen languages and with 470 contribu-tors from around the world.

Màrius (Serra) is a novelist, columnist and wordplay expert, whose cross-words for the *La Vanguardia* newspaper have become a national institution, and whose latest book, *Quiet [Still]*, an account both moving and unsenti-mental about life with his paralysed son, is currently a major best-seller here, with 25,000 copies sold in Catalan and 3,000 in Spanish (a Korean edition will be out soon).

Bernat (Puigtobella) is a publisher with a huge knowledge of Catalan, Hispanic, and Anglo-American literature whose finds include Joan-Daniel Bezsonoff from French Catalonia, Haruki Murakami, and two novelists who have yet to bring up a blip on the cultural radars of UK and US publish-ers: the German Juli Zeh and the Italian Niccolò Ammaniti. Among the books he is openly happiest about having published is *Animals tristos [Sad Animals]*, which was written by the person sitting beside him: Jordi (Puntí), who acquired his first readers back in 1998 when he published a well-received collection of stories called *Pell d'armadillo [Armadillo Skin]*. Four years later, he upped his literary ante to the point where not many other contemporary Catalan writers could see him, with the said *Sad Animals*, his second short-story collection which has since gone into French, German, Italian, Croatian, Spanish, and Portuguese. This post-Sant Jordi lunch was, as it happened, partially a celebration of Jordi's completion of his first novel, *Maletes perdudes [Lost Luggage]*, written in Barcelona, Munich, New York, Berlin, Copenhagen, London, and Tuscany over the previous six years: a book which the few who have read extracts of it talk about—with a glint of privilege in their eyes—as being objectively outstanding.

The coffees over, I felt my fun being spoiled by intimations of unreality, as it dawned on me for the umpteenth time that all I had to do was take a train ride out of Barcelona for a few hours in either direction—into monolingual

Spain or equally monolingual France and all the countries beyond—and I would be in a world which didn't so much as suspect the existence of the one in which these four people wrote and published. And even these four people—all this talent concentrated to the nth degree like a drop of Fairy Liquid in an old British TV ad—made up but a dash of the current Catalan cultural universe, of the plethora of products now being generated in song, poetry, fiction, theatre, TV, and drama, that happen to have the Catalan language as their trampoline.

So how can it be that if I, or anyone else, pops out of Catalonia and goes to any European capital, say, our local cultural news is (usually) met with reactions ranging from a dismissive "connais pas", to suspicious frowns or veiled references to the supposed provincialism and even "nationalism" (whatever that might exactly mean) of all things Catalan? How is it, indeed, that most of the planet never so much as even peeks at the sheer quality of so much Catalan culture today, at its international potential?

The reasons are no doubt many and varied, but one long-term foreign resident, the Argentinian journalist Patrícia Gabancho, believes firmly—as do increasing numbers of Catalans, if the statistics are anything to go by— that the area will remain bereft of any serious cultural recognition on any level, unless its political profile is raised considerably.

No wonder, given this state of affairs, that the best-selling non-fiction book in Catalan on Sant Jordi's Day was *Crònica de la Independència*, a hypothetical journalistic account of what would happen were Catalonia to obtain independence. Author, Patrícia Gabancho.

Oddly enough, none of my four table companions mentioned the book (although they all know Patrícia's work). Perhaps Catalonia has simply got to the stage where people now take for granted that foreign residents—writing in Catalan as a second language—can produce highly successful books dealing with controversial local issues, as if it were the most normal thing in the world. Which, like Catalonia itself, it very nearly is.

Found in Translation

El País, 2004 (as part of a series of English language
articles published in its cultural supplement)

American author Michael Zwerin, in *A Case For The Balkanisation Of Practically Everyone*—his 1976 study of several minority cultures around the world—dedicates a fair part of his chapter on Catalonia to a visit he made to a Barcelona bookstore. Checking out available titles in Catalan, he expected to find just a few local authors, and discovered to his amazement that a wide assortment of foreign writers, including Kerouac, Spillane, Camus, and Faulkner, were available in the language of Ramon Llull. This was all the more remarkable for being at the tail end of the Franco dictatorship, when Catalan language publishers were still hounded by the regime's censors. A year later, when democracy began to take root, these same publishers took advantage of their new-found freedom to step up the number of translations, to such an extent that, nowadays, readers in the Catalan speaking parts of Spain (and France, for that matter) enjoy direct access to a tremendous range of international literature, both classic and contemporary. Indeed, according to the prestigious translator Joan Sellent, in some genres over fifty per cent of books published in Catalan are translations (compared to an average figure of 3% for translations of foreign authors into English in the UK). No wonder, then, that on occasion the Catalan language reader is able to cock a snook at his counterparts abroad, by pointing to numerous examples of major authors whose books are more readily available in Catalan than in many far larger languages. Thanks to Monika Zgustova's exceptionally sensitive translations, for example, the work of Czech writer Bohumil Hrabal is easier to find in Barcelona's Casa del Llibre than it is in London's Foyles. More recently, *Necropolis*, an important novel by Slovenian Holocaust survivor Boris Pahor was published in Catalan. Curious English language readers, however, will search for it in vain on Amazon.

Literary translation into Catalan, it should be added, is not a recent development, having started in earnest in the 14th century, when the chancellery of the Catalano-Aragonese Federation began to encourage the translation of Latin works by Petrarch, Seneca, and Boethius, among others, into the vernacular. The following century even saw the translation of Dante's *Divine*

Comedy. By then, though, the Catalan speaking areas were slipping, largely for political reasons, into what historians call the Decadence—a cultural (and economic) slump lasting three centuries, during which few translations were published in Catalan. In the nineteenth century however, Catalonia received a new lease of life in the form of a movement for cultural revival known as the *Renaixença* (Renaissance), which promoted, among other things, the use of Catalan for literary purposes, translations included. One result of this was the creation of *L'Avenç*, a popular collection of cut-price books, by means of which the whole of European literature—from Homer and Molière to Ibsen and Nietzsche—was squeezed into the Catalan mindset over a thirty year period. This enterprise was complemented by the more exquisite project of the Bernat Metge Foundation, which sponsored the translation of Greek and Latin classics into Catalan. All this activity, needless to say, came to an abrupt end when fascist troops entered Barcelona in 1939, and Catalan became a virtually outlawed language. So much so, that mainstream publishing in Catalan did not pick up again until the 1960s, and even then, as we have seen, was subject to the whim of the censor. Today, however, despite having to get over the hurdles of several tricky stylistic debates, translation into Catalan is a going concern, with a pool of excellent translators to draw from. Even some books originally written in Spanish—like Javier Cercas's *Soldiers of Salamis* (2001)—have been translated successfully into Catalan, a remarkable recent phenomenon which, as far as I know, has no other parallel in Europe. Or can anyone imagine someone from Caernarvon reading Monica Ali, say, in Welsh?

ENDNOTE: Many thanks to Lea Lisjak for writing in—on February 24, 2008—with the following clarification: "Just thought you might be interested to know that the book *Nekropola* by Boris Pahor—that you mention in the article 'Found in Translation'—appeared in English under the title *Pilgrim among the shadows* (translated by Michael Biggins, published by Harcourt Brace & Company, 1995.)"

Graphic Examples

El País, 2004 (as part of a series of English language articles published in its cultural supplement)

In the early to mid 'Thirties—the heyday of the Second Republic, as popular with the people as it was loathed by the top two per cent—Barcelona was teeming with people, such as Josep Renau, Pere Català Pic and the legendary Carles Fontseré, who would now be called graphic designers but who at that time answered to the homelier title of "poster-makers". Their avant-garde advertising posters, with their bold designs and state-of-the-art photomontage techniques, were achieving European-wide recognition, but then—as is well-known—the top two per cent decided it couldn't bear to live in a republic any longer and gave a nod to the military, who dutifully plunged Spain into a notoriously brutal civil war. The poster-makers rallied to the republican cause, creating some of the finest graphic propaganda of the twentieth century (a well-known example is Fontseré's "Llibertat!", in which a black and red farm worker challenges the sky with an outsize scythe). Their efforts notwithstanding, the republic was eventually defeated, and, together with hundreds of thousands of other refugees, the mainstays of Barcelona's graphics boom went into exile. Francisco Franco, Spain's new dictator, was not a man known for his love of the decorative arts, and the more sinister aspects of his regime were accompanied by a general visual drabness, even in Barcelona as was recognised by some foreign visitors: "How dismal and woe-begone Barcelona looked," wrote Henry Miller in 1959.

It wasn't until the 1960s that things began to change on the design front, thanks in part to the work of lone entrepreneurs such as Antoni Morillas, who began by tarting up the labels on pharmaceutical packages and ended up founding Morillas & Associates, by far the largest graphic design company in the whole of Spain. It should be said, however, that Morillas' extraordinary career is not typical of that of most of Barcelona's contemporary graphic designers, whose work tends to be an idiosyncratic blend of the commercial and the creative, and who seem to prefer working from the designer equivalent of a garret rather than turning themselves into multinational enterprises. A perfect example of this is Peret, a world-class graphic designer who is also a fine illustrator and sculptor. At one stage, Peret owned a vast studio with a sizeable team of assistants on his payroll, but went back to working on his own: being a big-time boss, he claimed, stifled his creativity. This kind of integrity, closer to what you might expect from a notionally uncompromising artist rather than someone who lives off paid commissions, is a noticeable characteristic of the Barcelona design world.

Take Claret Serrahima, for example, another highly talented designer who has also decided to go it alone, even though that has meant leaving behind a design and packaging company, partly founded by himself, which has a turnover of millions of euros. Javier Mariscal, it is true, made a whole bunch of money in the 1990s and set up what amounted to a small industry in his Barcelona studio, but has retained, nonetheless, a simple, direct approach to his work. His friends Salvador Saura and Ramon Torrente were so determined to do their own thing, they mortgaged their houses in order to produce a series of stunning hand-bound books, complete with aluminium covers, exploding confetti, foam footprints and dozens of other visual surprises. Pioneers in their field, Saura and Torrente, like so many other Barcelona designers, started off with a wish and a prayer twenty odd years ago and are now at the peak of their careers, with all the creative freedom that their persistent individualism has allowed them. Theirs is the generation which has once again put Barcelona on the graphic design map, from which it was so violently ousted back in 1939. What is more, this time round no one is about to be sent into exile, so that graphic design in Barcelona, far from enjoying just a brief moment of glory, as it did before, now stands a reasonable chance of transforming itself into that happiest of paradoxes: a tradition with a future.

The Other Europe

El País, 2004 (as part of a series of English language
articles published in its cultural supplement)

There are fifty-eight native languages spoken in Europe, and just half
that number of states to speak them in. Which leaves us with an impres-
sive amount of what the European Union calls "regional and minority languages". These have several traits in common: first, they tend to be seen
as a threat to national unity by the state or states in which they are spoken, and have therefore been subject to relentless prohibition over many
years; second, the areas in which they are spoken are usually bilingual, due
to the imposition and/or adoption there of the official language of the state
in question; third, given that—as Barcelonan sociolinguist Carme Junyent
has pointed out—a bilingual situation will always lead to the elimination of
the weaker of the two languages, they are facing almost certain extinction in
either the short or the long term.

What options are open, then, for those members of stateless cultures
who have not resigned themselves to the demise of their own languages? One
possibility is to set up their own state, which is what the Latvians, Estonians,
and Lithuanians have done, all of them once linguistically marginalised on
their own territory by the overwhelming (and overbearing) presence of
Russian. There might, however, be a less radical option for regional-lan-
guage speakers in Europe: that of convincing the authorities, at the state
and European level, to concede political autonomy and consequent freedom
of linguistic use in bilingual territories. This is what has in fact happened,
albeit to some extent only, in the UK, Spain, Belgium, Luxembourg, and
several other countries, with differing degrees of success. These local initiatives, moreover, have been sanctioned by the 1992 European Charter for
Regional and Minority Languages, which the Council of Europe has urged
all EU members to sign. The intention is to bring the EU into line with the
international community, which has long recognised the equal status of all
languages, no matter how small, as well as the right of their speakers to use
them freely. Most of the EU countries duly signed—Spain (26% of whose
inhabitants speak a first language other than Spanish) rather reluctantly—
but there were two significant exceptions: Greece, and, above all, France.

Ken Hale, a linguist at the Massachusetts Institute of Technology, has declared, "Languages embody the intellectual wealth of the people who speak them. Losing any one of them is like dropping a bomb on the Louvre." To borrow Hale's imagery, then, it could be said that France has been zealously carpet-bombing its own minority languages for years, with a disregard for human culture frankly unbecoming to a democratic country. French-born speakers of Breton, Catalan, Corsican, Basque, Occitan, and other languages were humiliated and physically and mentally abused in French schools for generations, simply for using the language they spoke at home, a process which resulted in an incalculable number of psychological and cultural scars. (And still it goes on: just a month ago, for example, Georges Frêche, the socialist president of the Regional Council of Languedoc-Roussillon, publicly ridiculed the two non-French languages spoken in the area under his jurisdiction—Catalan and Occitan, each of them with a formidable literary history stretching back a thousand years—as *patois*).

However, large numbers of Europeans are refusing to let go of their regional mother tongues, no matter how often the powers that be—French and otherwise—bad-mouth them. The official influx of several small ex-regional languages (Slovenian, Slovakian, the above-mentioned Baltic vernaculars etc.) into the UE will give everyone food for thought. If most European states balk at the idea of ceding independence to the speakers of minority languages, they will surely have to face up to the fact that they are going to have to cede something to them, that they will at least have to openly celebrate and encourage rather than ignore or vilify the linguistic diversity of Europe. To do otherwise would be tantamount, many believe, to telling the stateless cultures within the UE that there is no middle path between statehood and oblivion.

Catalan: An International Language?

El País, 2004 (as part of a series of English language
articles published in its cultural supplement)

Back in 1978, Aina Moll, head of the Department of Linguistic Policy of the
newly restored *Generalitat* (Catalan Autonomous Government), made her
first attempt to redress the damage done to the Catalan language after nearly
forty years of Franco's fiercely nationalistic dictatorship, which had done
its level best to reduce Catalan—with its seven million speakers, its considerable literature, its widespread public use—to the status of a discredited
domestic *patois*. Moll knew that there was no point in harking back to the
pre-dictatorship days, when over 90% of the Catalan population spoke the
language, given that—the state's discriminatory anti-Catalan decrees apart—
a major linguistic shift had occurred with the arrival, in the fifties and sixties,
of a million and a half native Castilian speakers from other parts of Spain.

Moll realised that any attempt to get Catalan out of its post-Franco
quagmire would of necessity have to get these Castilian speakers actively
involved, hence the slogan of her first campaign: "Catalan is Everybody's
Business." To brighten up this campaign, her PR people came up with a
mascot: a manga-eyed little girl called Norma (named after the concept of
linguistic normalisation). Norma was shown, in a variety of cartoons, encouraging people to either use Catalan or to correct their Catalan. (Needless to
say, Norma soon became the butt of endless jokes, not least in the satirical
magazine *Culdesac*, which ran a strip called "Sub-Norma", in which Moll's
linguistic heroine tried to cajole prostitutes and drug dealers into catalanis-
ing their sales talk.) How effective was the Norma campaign? In the inimi-
table words of Bernat Puigtobella, in his article published here: "Norma is
a big girl now but she still hasn't had her period." Just so. Catalan may be
in a better situation than it was in 1978, but the general feeling is that is
hasn't yet matured into a fully normalised language. As a result, Catalonia—
Puigtobella *dixit*—lives in a state of permanent "linguistic hypochondria",
fuelled by a seemingly limitless number of pundits who regularly produce a

flurry of fretful articles, surveys and lectures on the language question, thus bringing on alternating fits of optimism or despondency (depending on the data released) among the Catalan-speaking population.

However, Puigtobella is quick to point out an interesting fact: internationally speaking, Catalan is on something of a roll, at least as far as the groves of academe are concerned, given that interested students can now learn Catalan at universities around the planet, from Australia to Argentina, from Israel to the Cameroon, from Morocco to Hungary. In Western Europe, Catalan is particularly well represented, with no less than 22 colleges teaching it in Germany, 20 in the UK, 10 in Italy and 9 in France. What, you might ask, could possibly induce foreign students to learn a relatively small, stateless language that, just thirty years ago, could land you in jail if you spoke it within hearing of the wrong policeman? It turns out there are a variety of reasons: the attraction of the exotic; the possibility of building an academic career in a field virtually bereft of competition; the chance to work as a tour guide in the Catalan speaking areas; free trips to the Balearics (in some cases); or, simply, the tremendous charisma exercised by some professors of Catalan, such as Alan Yates in Sheffield, or Tilbert Stegmann in Frankfurt. Whatever the reasons, the figures speak for themselves and Catalan has never been so widely taught abroad as it is now.

There is one fly in the ointment, though. Despite the fact that most linguists have for many years agreed that no language is intrinsically "better" than any other, there remain some who persist in regarding languages like Catalan (that is, not officially "national" languages in their respective states) as decidedly inferior. Which could be why in Spain (outside the Catalan-speaking areas) it is taught in a mere eight universities: that's 12 less than in the UK, and 14 less than in Germany. Clearly, Norma never made it to Madrid.

Hard Times

A review of *The Enormity of the Tragedy,*
Quim Monzó's first novel to be published in English

The Times Literary Supplement, 16 November 2007

Some ten years ago, the host on Catalan public television's then most popular chat show asked Quim Monzó how he thought a stable couple might be affected if one of its members had a fling. Ignoring the question, Monzó snapped back: "There are no stable couples", a retort that would not have taken his readers as much aback as it visibly did the presenter, used as they already were to Monzó's fictional presentation of life as a kind of quirky video game in which anything can happen and everything is, therefore, provisional.

In the opening chapters of *The Enormity of the Tragedy*, Monzó toys with this conditional view of things to comic effect: a failed publisher turned trumpet player, Ramon-Maria, and the woman he is trying to seduce, Maria-Eugènia, go from a restaurant (in which he has drunk too much champagne) to a bar where he tries to sober himself up with a coffee, worried that he won't be able to get an erection in the likely event one will soon be required. She has a brandy to keep him company. He finishes his coffee too fast and, as she is only half-way through her brandy, orders a rum-cola to keep her company. The rum-cola is delayed, so that when it arrives, she has finished her brandy but orders another to keep him company. And so it goes on until Ramon-Maria finds himself negotiating the steps to her flat, "completely plastered". A beautifully timed sequence that has the reader finding it all but impossible not to laugh his (or her) head off.

Easy as it would have been to maintain this lightly humorous tone, Monzó immediately ups the narrative ante by giving Ramon-Maria, predictably afflicted with a droop, a huge erection that refuses to go away, no matter what. We then meet the story's other main character, Ramon-Maria's stepdaughter, Anna-Francesca, a fifteen year-old assailed by successive waves of self-centred puppy love. A second plot twist—to explain which would spoil the book for first-time readers—pushes both Ramon-Maria and

Anna-Francesca into respective spirals of despair and murderous spite. The outcome is a tragedy as cruel as it is telling: the dark side of the title's apparently flippant sexual pun.

Monzó occasionally twists his own distinctive style into brief pastiches of Shakespearean bluster, Loompanics murder manuals, teen magazine stories, and even certain well-known Barcelonan novelists whose use of the city in their fiction verges on a pandering to potential tourists. Hence Monzó's European reputation as a genius of "postmodern literary parody" (to quote the English blurb).

Happily, he is a great deal more. To read this novel is to enter the fictional universe of an author trapped permanently between astonishment and aversion at the world he has found himself in, so estranged that his only possible literary recourse is an almost manic humour underpinned by a frighteningly bleak vision of the day-to-day, both conveyed to the full by Monzó's painstakingly precise use of language—in his case, the Catalan language—finely rendered by Peter Bush.

The Enormity Of The Tragedy—notwithstanding its debts to Robert Coover, John Cheever, surrealist Sabadell writer Francesc Trabal and the Mexico-exiled Catalan master of magical realism, Pere Calders, among others—is a thoroughly original piece of writing and a venerable modern classic in its own country. Let us hope that Monzó's latest book, *Mil Cretins [A Thousand Cretins]*, published in October 2007, will not have to wait quite so long—nearly two decades—for an English translation.

The Enormity of the Tragedy by Quim Monzó. Translated from the Catalan by Peter Bush. Peter Owen Publishers, London, 2007. 222 pages. Fiction. ISBN: 978-0-7206-1299-8

(Note: I have maintained the original title and text of this review. The version published in the *Times Literary Supplement* was altered slightly for reasons of space.)

Autumn of the Patriarch

A review of Najat El Hachmi's novel
The Last Patriarch

The Times Literary Review, 1 August 2008

The Catalan literary world is still reeling from the jolt it received earlier this year when the Ramon Llull Prize—the most prestigious of all Catalan-language fiction awards—was granted to Najat El Hachmi, a twenty-eight-year-old Moroccan-born woman, who had only begun writing fiction in Catalan in her teens. At first, to her disgust (she considers herself as Catalan as the next citizen), an enormous media meal was made of what were referred to as her *immigrant origins*. Slowly, however, attention shifted from the supposedly anomalous nature of the author to her novel itself, *L'últim patriarca [The Last Patriarch]*.

It is divided into two sections of equal length. In the first, the (never named) protagonist describes the formation and upbringing of her father, Mimoun Driouch, in a (never specified) Berber-speaking region of Morocco. Keeping her narrative distance by means of an ironic commentary written in a skilfully quasi-oral style, the narrator goes on to describe how her father leaves his home in North Africa for a small Catalan town, finds work and a lover there, and, having been pressured by his daughter—"Why don't you leave that Christian whore and take care of us for a change?", she tells him on the phone—finally decides to allow his wife and children to come and live with him in Catalonia.

The ostensibly detached panoramic chronicle of Part One is replaced in Part Two by the literary equivalent of a permanent close-up. Here, the daughter places herself in the narrative limelight in order to reveal the true nature of her father, who turns out to be a jealous paranoiac who has convinced himself, against all evidence, that his wife has been unfaithful to him back in Morocco and that his once beloved daughter is nothing but a potential prostitute.

If the first part is a fine, wry look at a man and his background which minces no words when describing his personal hardships (it is suggested, for example, that when still a teenager, Mimoun was raped by an uncle), the

Matthew Tree

second part dunks the reader into the claustrophobic horror of life with this would-be patriarch, who nearly stabs his wife, beats up his daughter in public, and does his best to control every detail of their lives.

This second half of *L'últim patriarca* is a tour de force: a graphic account of a young woman's coming of age in a Catalan rural town, with references as diverse as Jean-Claude Van Damme, Super Mario, Zadie Smith, the Catalan novelist Mercè Rodoreda, and Erich Fromm floating through her emergent cultural universe as she tries to cope all the time with her unhinged father. The fact that El Hachmi describes her main character's plight in individualistic rather than collective terms—thus sidestepping the clichés that occasionally dog what some universities have dubbed *Immigrant Lit*—allows her to evoke emotions in the reader that have no ethnic strings attached, right through to the denouement.

Waiting for the Break

An article on Catalan literature,
past and present

The Times, April 23, 1999

In 1979, a British publisher scrawled "There is simply no readership here for regional literature", over the unread MS of a translated Catalan novel (Manuel de Pedrolo's *All the Beasts of Burden*). One more example, if one were needed, that to be classified as "regional" is to be relegated to the ranks of the thoroughly undesirable, in publishing terms. Catalan literature, incredibly, has suffered for decades—if not centuries—from this dreaded "regional" label.

Incredibly, because Catalan has more speakers (seven and a half million) than several official European languages, covers a wide area (Valencia, Spanish Catalonia, French Catalonia, Andorra, southern Aragon, the Balearic Islands) and its literary output is comparable to that of several larger languages. Unfortunately, many factors have contributed over the years to distort the true nature of Catalan language and literature. It was incorporated into the Spanish State by force of arms in the early 18th century and the Catalan-speaking areas were subjected for over two hundred and fifty years to a series of laws designed to suppress the public use of Catalan—books included—culminating in a vicious attempt to completely eliminate the language in the early phases of the Franco dictatorship (a very small literary leeway was allowed it after 1962).

Under democracy, Catalan writing still has to contend with considerable antipathy from the Spanish reading public to Catalan language authors (testified to by many Barcelona publishers)—a considerable disadvantage given that foreign publishers tend to judge Catalan books exclusively on their sales in Spanish translation. And the aggressive indifference shown to matters Catalan by many of the Cervantes Institutes (or Spanish cultural embassies) around the world, certainly doesn't help. No wonder the British publisher didn't bother to read the book.

Matthew Tree

Had he done so, however, he would have found that *All the Beasts of the Burden* was a brilliant, highly disturbing political fantasy, whose author, Manuel de Pedrolo, had over 140 titles to his credit, ranging from best-selling science and detective fiction to poetry and existential drama. His appetite duly whetted, the publisher might then have gone on to check out other major works of Catalan literature, from Joanot Martorell's *Tirant lo Blanc*, arguably the first great European novel, or Ausiàs March's 15th century love poetry, which foreshadows Romantic individualism by four centuries. He could have chanced on the surrealist poetry of Salvat-Papasseit and J.V. Foix, both major influences on the work of Dalí and Miró, respectively, or stumbled across the extraordinary novels of Mercè Rodoreda that appeared in the 1960s or Josep Pla's unbeatable descriptions of Catalan and European life spanning fifty years (and collected in sixty volumes) or Pere Calder's beautifully crafted short-stories of the 1970s. Etc. etc. etc. But he didn't: "No readership here..."

Neither has the situation changed since the exposure provided by the 1992 Olympic Games turned Barcelona into the fourth most visited city in Europe. Take an important contemporary writer like Quim Monzó, whose fourteen works of fiction and non-fiction, all of which are still in print, have had total sales of over 600,000 books in Catalan alone, with many titles running into as many as twenty-five editions. Already translated into eleven languages, and described by an American critic as "the best European short story writer in the last decade", Mr Monzó—together with many other excellent contemporary authors such as Carme Riera and Miquel Bauçà—remains inexplicably unavailable to the English reading public.

Help, however, is on its way. Since Catalan was allowed to be taught properly in the schools (1984), more and more people living in the areas where the language is spoken are now able to read and write it with ease, and as a result Catalan book production has inched up over the years until it now accounts for no less than 12% of all book publishing in Spain (6,000 new titles a year).

On top of this, the success of Catalan public television (market leader for the last five years) has helped create a literary mass-market for the first time ever, with books like TV presenter Andreu Buenafuente's three collections of monologues, published at the turn of the century, selling over 100,000 copies each. This commercially healthy panorama is being enhanced on a more serious level by a new generation of European-class authors, such as poet Enric Cassasas and gifted fiction writers like Albert Sánchez, Imma Monsó, and Jordi Puntí. In a nutshell, Catalan writing, past and present, has never been in a better position to break out of the "regional" cocoon imposed on it by politics and prejudice, finally giving foreign readers a chance to discover a major national literature which has been one of Europe's best kept secrets for far too long.

Matthew Tree

Laughter in the Light

On Henry Miller in Barcelona

Barcelona Ink, 29 December 2010

When Henry Miller stopped off in Barcelona in late April of 1953, during a European tour, he was in a situation both enviable and depressing. Although, at age 62, he had long been acclaimed by many fellow writers, and some literary critics, around the world as one of the 20th century's most important living authors, the books on which this reputation rested (*Tropic of Cancer, Black Spring, Tropic of Capricorn, Sexus* and *Plexus*) could not be published in any English-speaking country, whose censors, prudes to a man (none were women), objected strongly to Miller's strong language. In Germany, Denmark, Sweden, and Japan, though, these same books were freely available in translation. In France, and France alone, the unexpurgated English versions had been on the open market since Miller wrote them (in Paris, in the 1930s) thanks to a curious loophole in Gallic law, which at that time banned all obscene books as long as they were in French, giving other, presumably less serious, languages a free erotic rein. In Britain and the US, his readers had to make do with that handful of his titles which were unsullied by rude words and ruder episodes, such as the collection of essays *The Cosmological Eye* (New York, 1939) or his chaste book about Greece, *The Colossus of Maroussi*, which sold 50,000 copies in the UK alone, when published in 1950.

Miller lived in California—in a shack on Big Sur—and his European and Japanese royalties were arriving infrequently, irregularly and in quantities too small to live on. Especially complicated was the situation with the French royalties, which had been accumulating considerably over the years, but which were unavailable to Miller due to currency export restrictions. His friend Lawrence Durrell had urged him to buy somewhere in France and move there, before the French government devalued the franc, an imminent economic measure which would have wiped out Miller's small French fortune. That was one reason for Miller's trip to Europe in the early 1950s; the other being that most of his closest friends—whom he had not seen since his Paris days—lived there. On top of which he had just separated from his third wife and started up a relationship with the woman who would end up being his fourth: Eve McClure, a young, long time admirer of his work. So the European trip, which was to last seven months, also became a kind of extended honeymoon.

The first stop, unsurprisingly, was Paris, the city in which Miller had found his written voice twenty years earlier. After hobnobbing it with the painter Fernand Léger and the photographers Man Ray and Brassaï, and having been greeted with a flurry of enthusiastic articles about his work in the French Press, Henry and Eve moved on to Brussels, which neither of them had visited before. (Miller, having observed the Belgians for a few days, concluded they were "neither fish nor fowl, more like potato balls".) They then crossed the French Midi and drove into Spain, where Miller had one overriding objective: to meet up with his oldest and closest friend, Alfred Perlès, in Barcelona, after a separation of thirteen years.

Alfred Perlès was an Austrian-born writer (his parents were Czech Jews) who Miller had briefly met during an exploratory visit to Paris in 1928. Two years later, Miller had settled in Paris without a penny to his name, and was sitting one day on the terrace of the Dôme café, drinking brandy after brandy in order to drum up enough Dutch courage to tell the waiter he couldn't pay for them, when Perlès came across him quite by chance, settled the bill, and invited him to move into his rented flat. (Perlès, unlike Miller, had an income, being a proof-reader for the Paris edition of the *Herald Tribune*.) Together with the young Lawrence Durrell and Anaïs Nin, Perlès would form part of Miller's Parisian inner circle in the years 1930 to 1938.

This was the period that saw the publication of much of Miller's finest autobiographical work, in some of which—*Tropic of Cancer* and *Quiet Days In Clichy*—Perlès himself plays a prominent part (under the pseudonym "Carl"). Their close friendship was to last until Miller's death in 1980, but went through its shakiest patch precisely in the years before the reunion in Barcelona. Since the 1930s, Perlès had renounced his anarchistic and pacifist views, had moved to England, married, settled down (in Wells, in the county of Somerset) and had enlisted in the British Army during the Second World War. Miller saw this as a kind of betrayal of what he saw as Perlès's true self, and grim though the Catalan capital must have been in 1953, I can't help suspecting that if this meeting had been in, say, Brussels or Brooklyn, they wouldn't have felt quite so free to laugh quite so much. Barcelona, at least, is on the Mediterranean.

i

be:

too

kn

t

th

an

Pa

lo

'

About the Author

Matthew Tree was born in London at the tail end of 1958. He has lived in Barcelona since 1984. For literary reasons of his own, in 1990 he stopped writing in English and switched to Catalan, in which language he has so far published ten books, including two novels, a collection of short stories, an autobiography, two books on Catalonia, a rant against work, and a personal essay on racism. In English he has published *What's Barcelona?* (with photographs by Txema Salvans) and *Barcelona, Catalonia*. In 2000, he began writing in English again, in which language he completed a novel, *Private Country*, and a slice of autobiography, *Calling Card*, extracts of which have been published in various literary magazines in Scotland, Canada, and Catalonia. He has a regular column in the *Avui* newspaper and the magazine *Catalonia Today*, and is also an occasional contributor to *The Times Literary Supplement*. He is currently putting the finishing touches to a new novel in English.

For more information: *http://www.matthewtree.cat/index.php?idioma=eng* or Antonia Kerrigan Literary Agency (*http://www.antoniakerrigan.com*)

Lightning Source UK Ltd.
Milton Keynes UK
UKOW050137100712

195718UK00001B/89/P